In this collection of essay[...] [pro]vocative, hysterical best. [...] [...] always enlightening and always an event. I loved the previous collections of his articles and enjoyed this one just as much. These chapters will edify, entertain, and occasionally infuriate. What more could one ask for in a book?

— **Kevin DeYoung,** Senior Pastor, University Reformed Church, East Lansing, Michigan

Though he might not take himself too seriously, Carl Trueman takes the gospel very seriously in this wonderful little book. Trueman offers laugh-out-loud, insightful commentary on theology, culture, the church, and the Christian life. His rapier wit cuts through absurdity and bad theology like a hot knife through butter. This is Trueman at his best, using "humor in the service of theology."

— **J. V. Fesko,** Academic Dean and Associate Professor of Systematic and Historical Theology, Westminster Seminary California

The essay used to be a key subgenre of Christian writing (witness those of the Baptist John Foster or the Catholic G. K. Chesterton), but in recent days the art of the essayist has become something of a lost art among evangelicals. As this scintillating collection of mini-essays clearly reveals, however, past essayists like Foster and Chesterton have a worthy successor in Trueman. His essays are not always easy to read—not so much because of the difficulty of their content but due to their distinct prophetic edge. Like the essays of Foster and Chesterton, however, although Tureman's essays do not always soothe, they do ultimately edify.

— **Michael A. G. Haykin,** The Southern Baptist Theological Seminary, Louisville

Wit and wisdom don't always go together with theologians, especially with historical theologians. When they do, it's a real treat. Proving the adage that those who don't understand history are doomed to repeat it, Carl Trueman brings the treasures of the past to bear on the challenges and opportunities of the present. Even if you don't agree with everything he says, you can't help but be provoked to ponder God, yourself, the church, and our culture in fresh ways.

—*Michael Horton,* J. Gresham Machen Professor of Theology, Westminster Seminary California

The Reverend Rodney Trotter is an international treasure, and his current residence in Cricklewood belies his ambition to address theological concerns on a global scale. The man seems fearless, offending sacred cows of all sizes and types. His writings shake the very foundations of conservative theological empires. I fully expect him to be named as *Time* magazine's "Most Influential Theologian" any day now.

—*Derek W. H. Thomas,* Minister of Preaching and Teaching, First Presbyterian Church, Columbia, South Carolina; Distinguished Visiting Professor of Systematic and Historical Theology, Reformed Theological Seminary, Jackson, Mississippi

FOOLS RUSH IN

WHERE MONKEYS FEAR TO TREAD

Taking Aim at Everyone

CARL R. TRUEMAN

P U B L I S H I N G

P.O. BOX 817 • PHILLIPSBURG • NEW JERSEY 08865-0817

Printed in the United States of America

Library of Congress Cataloging-in-Publication Data

Trueman, Carl R.
 Fools rush in where monkeys fear to tread : taking aim at everyone / Carl R. Trueman.
   p. cm.
 Includes bibliographical references.
 ISBN 978-1-59638-405-7 (pbk.)
 1. Christianity and culture. I. Title.
 BR115.C8T78 2011
 261--dc23

                        2011047702

To
Sandy Finlayson
and
Paul Levy
"The laughter is on our side."

CONTENTS

CONTENTS

FOREWORD

The Reverend Rodney Trotter

IT IS AN UNUSUAL HONOR to be invited to write a preface for this collection of writings by my childhood friend and erstwhile verbal sparring partner, Carl Trueman. I remember some years ago, Carl telling me that Ian Thompson, then working at another Christian publishing firm, had described an earlier compilation of his writings, *The Wages of Spin*, as a book without a theme, without a constituency, and thus without a market. Well, Ian is now working for P&R Publishing and faced with a dilemma of similar provenance: selling another of Trueman's books that, if anything, is even less coherent than its ancestor.

The essays, aphorisms, and brief jottings in this book are not united by any internal theme beyond being reflections, whether direct, satirical, or merely subversive, of contemporary Western and particularly American culture, especially as it bleeds into the Christian world and receives inadequate responses therein. To the literal-minded, there is much here that will simply confuse; to those who prefer to use emoticons rather than whole sentences with built-in irony, I would simply suggest that you look elsewhere for inspiration.

Mockery is both powerful and important within the church, not as a means to belittle others but as a means to belittle all. The Bible itself contains numerous passages of deep irony and mockery, with the lessons expressed in such passages made powerful as much by this form as by their content. One thinks of Psalm 115, where the idolaters become as impotent and as fake as the idols they have manufactured; or Isaiah 44, where the man chops down a tree, uses half of the timber to cook his meal, and bows down and worships the other half; or even God's pointed and painful mockery of Jonah through his destruction of the gourd. In each case, the irony of the text is part and parcel of its power.

Humor has been lost on most Protestant writers. For some reason, the funniest and most ironic theological writing tends to come from the Catholics: Newman, Chesterton, Belloc, and, in recent days, Percy and Neuhaus. Yet it was not always the case. Protestantism was not always the preserve of the humorless, the dessicated, the self-important, and the professionally hurting and offended. The founder of the feast, Martin Luther, understood the power of humor, probably because he understood the absurdity of human self-regard in the context of the fallen world. He showed no mercy, either to his enemies or indeed to himself on this score. His writings are an oasis of welcome wit in the desert of Protestant pomposity.

Today, as always, there is a ridiculously pretentious dimension to fallen human beings, a risible tendency to assume that we are important not simply to our immediate family and friends, but to all. This unfortunate bias toward what is, in effect, self-worship has only been enhanced and exacerbated by the advent of the exhibitionism of the web, of blogs, of Facebook, and of a myriad other "social networking" outfits. Such bubbles of pretention need to be burst; but how to do it, without falling prey to the same? Trueman's answer has been to use the very tools such media provide to mock everything, the author himself included. Whether he always—or, indeed, ever—succeeds in this, I leave to the reader to decide; but he has certainly tried. Taste in humor, like preferences in sport, is, after all, a deeply subjective and irrational thing: one either intuitively grasps it, or one does not.

A custard pie in the face is the funniest thing one man has ever seen; to another, it is a degrading act of physical assault. This book is, I suspect, designed to be enjoyed by the former, and to offend the latter. Enjoy—or abominate—as you wish. In today's world—I mean "church"—the customer, after all, is indeed king.

Rodney Trotter, M.A. (Cantab.)
Theologian-in-Residence
Pastoral Centre for the Creative Arts
Cricklewood
The Feast Day of St. Olaf the
Sublime
January 2011

ACKNOWLEDGMENTS

I AM INDEBTED TO Marvin Padgett and Ian Thompson, of P&R Publishing, and to Robert Brady, of the Alliance of Confessing Evangelicals, for suggesting the idea of this book, and to Gabe Fluhrer, Executive Editor of *Reformation 21*, for preliminary editing and manuscript preparation. I am also grateful to John J. Hughes and the staff at P&R Publishing for bringing the project through the final stages of editing and production and, in particular, to Brian Kinney for his careful editing of the manuscript. Finally, I wish to thank Amanda Martin and Ron Evans at P&R Publishing for creating the excellent Discussion Questions found at the end of this volume.

Editor's Note. Some chapters conclude with excerpts from Carl's blog posts. These excerpts follow a decorative element and are set as block quotes.

FOOLS RUSH IN WHERE MONKEYS FEAR TO TREAD

December 2009

SOME WEEKS AGO a friend forwarded me a link to the blog of an American Christian academic. Now, at the risk of protesting too much, I must stress that I don't read blogs—I really don't read blogs—unless, that is, they are sent to me by someone else. Sufficient to my own life is the tedium and banality contained therein; I really have no interest in compounding such with the tedium and banality contained in the lives of other people.

This blog, however, caught my eye, not so much for the specific post to which I had been referred, but because, as I glanced in boredom at the various other posts this person had archived, I noted that part of the stock-in-trade of this particular chap was criticism of Reformed evangelicals as smug and arrogant. This did not bother me, nor did the lack of imagination: hitting the Reformed in such a way in today's Emergent circles is a bit like calling Obama a "Marxist" in a speech to a branch meeting of the

John Birch Society—you may not actually know what you are talking about, but the crowd will love it, and you certainly won't have to buy your own drinks at the bar afterward.

What amused me was not the obvious playing to the gallery; no, what was so funny was the self-description in the little bar off to the side, where I was assured that the gent concerned was "a widely-recognized authority" in his own field, a "witty speaker," and a figure of some importance, with appearances everywhere from national radio and TV to local churches. The irony was clearly lost on the author—railing against Reformed smugness on one half of the web page, while describing himself as a very witty and important person on the other; but, hey, sensitivity to the ironic is generally not a strong point of the Earnest But "Witty" Progressive Brigade.

Now, it is one thing to have others write commendations of you for a book cover or conference brochure—perhaps necessary evils in the cut-throat world of publishing and conferences; and nobody should believe them, least of all the objects of such patent flannel; but to say it about yourself implies that you might actually believe the propaganda, that maybe you yourself are just a wee bit arrogant and smug. And, remember, this chap wasn't even Reformed. I shudder to think how much worse he might be if he endorsed the Westminster Standards or the Three Forms of Unity. One can only assume that the kind of man who describes himself on his own website as "witty" is likely to be the same kind of man who laughs at his own jokes and, quite probably, applauds himself at the end of his own speeches—behavior that was previously the exclusive preserve of politicians, Hollywood stars, and chimpanzees.

Yet this example is just one more piece of Christian absurdity in this topsy-turvy world where anything is now possible. What next, I wonder? Will black become white? Will the pope cease to be Catholic? Will woodland bears start to use public conveniences? And will Dutch people start listing Belgium as their first choice destination for holidays? Indeed, on the same day I received the above link, I was directed by another friend to a website where an individual had put up on a social network page a public announcement that he was "humbled" by a reference to himself or herself on a well-known theologian's blog. Curiouser and curiouser, I thought: being humbled usually involves becoming more self-effacing, making oneself more invisible, bringing less attention to oneself. At least, that's what the Oxford Dictionary implies; but, hey-ho, maybe Webster's is different?

This person had no doubt asked himself how he might best demonstrate this self-effacement. "Perhaps I should send a private note of thanks to the person concerned, expressing quiet appreciation for his kind reference to me," he no doubt reflected; but then, suddenly, a light bulb must have clicked on in his head—"No. I know what I'll do. I'll announce my humility on my Facebook page! Surely it is hard to imagine a more humble and less attention-seeking move? And, yes, while I'm logged on, I'll also mention it on the very web page where said well-known theologian originally puffed me, just to make sure that everybody knows how humbled I truly am."

Don't laugh—this really happened, and, what's more, the absurdity of the story does not end there. The well-known theologian's website to which our humble friend had taken us also contained a link to another person's site, this time to a recorded interview with—guess who?—the well-known theologian himself! The subject? The importance of the books written by himself! 'Tis true—for you could not possibly make this stuff up.

But the sordid tales of the inverted morality of the Christian web are seemingly limitless. The self-absorption on display here called to my mind yet another web page I am sometimes directed to visit by friends, where the only subject ever discussed seems to be the author's own contribution to Christian thought, and, very occasionally, the critical interaction of others with his earth-shattering insights (none of his critics understand him and are generally idiots or wicked or both). As one colleague describes said page: see me here, hear me there, stroke my ego everywhere. Indeed, this page always brings to my mind the tale of the apocryphal Cambridge don who used to warble on and on about himself in tutorials until one day, in a moment of humility, he turned to his hapless students and declared, "Well, that's enough about me; let's talk about you for a change. What do you think of my books?" But then the owner of this website is a "leading scholar," a claim that must be true because he himself tells us so on his very own web page; and he should know because he is, after all, a "leading scholar." And you thought the noise at a chimpanzee's tea party could be deafening.

Let's stop there a minute. This is madness. Is this where we have come with our Christian use of the web? Men who make careers in part out of bashing the complacency and arrogance of those with whose theology they disagree, yet who applaud themselves on blogs and twitters they have built solely for their own deification? Young men who are so humbled by flattering references that they just have to spread the word of their contribution all over the web like some dodgy rash they picked up in the tropics? And established writers who are so insecure that they feel the need to direct others to places where they are puffed and pushed as the next big thing? I repeat: this is madness, stark staring, conceited, smug, self-glorifying madness of the most pike-staffingly obvious and shameful variety.

But yet there is more. There is another phenomenon on web pages that seems closely akin to these direct puffs of one's own greatness; and that is greatness by proxy. Sufferers of this syndrome develop the uncontrollable habit of continually using the language of intimate friendship about everybody who is perceived to be anybody, thereby making themselves seem to be close to the movers and shakers of the theological world. In such conversations and on such blogs, contacts of only recent and superficial vintage are referenced familiarly as "Dave" or "Geoff" or "my mate, Kev." With such people, every passing acquaintance is an intellectual intimate; and names casually picked up at lunch, by nightfall are intentionally dropped on personal blog sites, as every pushy arriviste and aspiring parvenu strains to project an image of inner-circle savvy to their needy blog followers.

This is truly a land beyond satire. It is the very antithesis of the attitude of an agnostic lady I knew in the nineteen-eighties who, when asked where her son went to university, would always reply, "Oh, to a small college in East Anglia," because she feared that the more precise explanation—the University of Cambridge—would bring too much attention to her family and be seen as a way of puffing up herself and belittling others. She was truly modest and fiercely private. Such a different attitude to the "me first and only" exhibitionism found on the web—the Christian web!—today. As I said, book blurbs are one thing; but here we have a world where we have not just eliminated the middle man by producing the phenomenon of the self-blurber; we have then taken it one stage further—we have eliminated the need for the very book whose existence was, traditionally, the necessary precondition of such a blurb. All that is left is the Onanistic self-aggrandizement of those who proclaim themselves "humble" and "witty," and "leading scholars." Sheer virtual Onanism. No wonder their eyesight is so bad they seem blind to their problem.

Now, none of us should be arrogant and complacent about this. I am always mindful of the great line from *Seven Pillars of Wisdom*, when T. E. Lawrence refers to his own ambivalence to public acclaim: "There was a craving to be famous; and a horror of being known to like being known." Lawrence clearly struggled with fame; and even more so with the fear that his enjoyment of fame might become known; but let's remember how high the bar was set for him. He had, after all, led the Arab Revolt and was one of the few people who could be justifiably described as a living legend; his work, military and literary, was truly monumental; he hadn't just launched a blog page where he could talk about "my old buddy, Big Winnie" and "my beers with Gertrude," and post pics with captions such as "Here's one of me in Damascus with Faisal and the lads."

If Lawrence had real grounds for his struggle because he had really achieved significance, the same is surely not true for any of us. We mediocrities struggle at a different level, hoping that our own petty contributions, irrelevant and ephemeral as they are, will be puffed up and acknowledged by others; and, in a sense, there is nothing we can do about that. I am a man divided against myself; I want to be the center of attention because I am a fallen human being; I want others to know that I am the special one; and as long as the new me and the old me are bound together in a single, somatic unity, I will forever be at war with myself. What I can do, however, is have the decency to be ashamed of my drive to self-promotion and my craving for attention and for flattery and not indulge it as if it were actually a virtue or a true guide to my real merit. I am not humble, so I should not pretend to be so but rather confess it in private, seeking forgiveness and sanctification. And, negatively, I must avoid doing certain things. I must not proudly announce my humility on the Internet so that all can gasp in wonder at my self-effacement. I must make sure I never refer to myself as a scholar. I must not tell people how wonderful I am. I must resist the temptation to laugh at my own jokes. I must not applaud my own speeches. I must deny myself the pleasure of posting other people's overblown flattery of me on my own website, let alone writing such about myself. I must never make myself big by clinging to the coattails of another. In short, I must never take myself too seriously. Not even chimpanzees do that.

Some weeks back I noted a leading Emergent web page that spends its time telling the reader how important and radical (in the Starbucks latte drinking sense of the word) the particular person who writes on it is. I raised the question of how, in the marketplace of ideas, Christians can promote the good and the true without promoting themselves. In this context, I'm struck by the following comment from good old P. T. Forsyth, scarcely a conservative evangelical but a whole lot wiser than the Emergent person on said website, and any who are tempted to think too highly of themselves, whatever their theological conviction: "The work of the ministry labors under one heavy disadvantage when we regard it as a profession and compare it with other professions. In these, experience brings facility, a sense of mastery in the subject, self-satisfaction, self-confidence; but in our subject the more we pursue it, the more we enter into it, so much the more are we cast down with the overwhelming sense, not only of our insufficiency, but of our unworthiness. Of course, in the technique of our work we acquire a certain ease. We learn to speak more or less freely and aptly. We learn the knack of handling a text, of conducting church work, or dealing with men, and the like. If it were only texts or men we had to handle! But we have to handle the gospel. We have to lift up Christ—a Christ who is the death of natural self-confidence—a humiliating, even a crushing Christ; and we are not always alive to our uplifting and resurrection in Him. We have to handle a gospel that is a new rebuke to us every step we gain in intimacy with it. There is no real intimacy with the gospel that does not mean a new sense of God's holiness, and it may be long before we realize that the same holiness that condemns is that which saves. There is no new insight into the cross that does not bring, whatever else come with it, a deeper sense of the solemn holiness of the love that meets us there. And there is no new sense of the holy God that does not arrest His name upon our unclean lips. If our very repentance is to be repented of, and we should be forgiven much in our very prayers, how shall we be proud, or even pleased, with what we may think a success in our preaching? So that we are not surprised that some preachers, after what the public calls a most brilliant and impressive discourse, retire . . . to humble themselves before God, to ask forgiveness for the poor message, and to call themselves most unprofitable servants—yea, even when they knew themselves that they had "done well." The more we grasp our gospel the more it abashes us.[1]

If PTF is on target, then the kind of self-promotion in which evangelicals, emergent, Reformed, whatever, routinely indulge speaks volumes about our grasp of the holiness of God, the truly radical nature of the gospel, and the stupidity of any attitude on our part other than humility. Web page self-promotionists beware!

1. P. T. Forsyth, *The Soul of Prayer* (Grand Rapids: Eerdmans, n.d.), 71.

2

THE CROWD IS UNTRUTH

July 2010

THE GREAT DANISH theologian and philosopher, Søren Kierkegaard, is probably best known in Christian circles for his haunting reflections on God's command to Abraham to sacrifice his son, Isaac. While I am guessing many of us would question the theology that underlies some of Kierkegaard's exegesis of the passage, I think there are few Christian writers or preachers who have so ably captured the terror and confusion that must have filled Abraham's mind as he made the lonely journey to the place of sacrifice.

Kierkegaard is not easy to read at the best of times; some of his longer works are, to put it very bluntly, surely among the most tedious masterpieces ever penned. Who, I wonder, except for the most infatuated fan, has ever plowed through all of the stages on life's way recounted in the book of the same name (*Stages on Life's Way*)? Further, his appropriation by later existentialist philosophy has had the twofold effect of making him a rather suspect character among the ranks of the orthodox, an irrelevance to philosophers trained in Anglo-American circles, and a quaint figure of yester-year to the vanguard of the latest continental philosophical ideas. Indeed, I remember as a young Christian finding his journals particularly interesting, and then reading Francis Schaeffer and realizing that SK should really be placed in the "debit" column; I was thus one of those whom James Barr characterized as not having to think because Schaeffer had done my thinking for me.

Yet, over the years, I have returned to SK again and again, and not just because I found a compulsive need to think for myself and to resist letting Schaeffer—or any of the other evangelical gurus—do it for me. Partly the pleasure of reading SK arises from the fact that his one-liners are virtually without peer. Indeed, if you are as bone-idle as I am, you have to love any man who can come up with a statement such as "Far from idleness being the root of all evil, it is rather the only true good" (*Either/Or*). And I even possess a mug with the inscription, "The truth shall set ye free; but first it shall make ye miserable." If ever there was a sentiment of which a Northern European, living in the oversized Disney World that is the U.S.A., needed to keep reminding himself, it is surely that one. Indeed, among the few pleasures left to me now that my children are teenagers and regard me with withering disdain, and being a pessimist trapped in a nation of chirpy optimists, is in the bleak landscapes of SK's essays and the films of Ingmar Bergman. I need my misery.

But there are other reasons for reading SK, perhaps most of all his unnerving ability to nail aspects of society that have actually become more significant since his death rather than less. Here, it is some of his shorter, lesser-known essays that contain some of his most brilliant and penetrating insights. One of them in particular, *The Crowd Is Untruth*, is both profound and prophetic. In it, he captures brilliantly both the power of the anonymity of the crowd, where personal responsibility, accountability, and identity are surrendered to the larger group. He pinpoints that which became all too tragically true in the subsequent century, the ease with which a talented person can manipulate a crowd into doing the most terrible things. Crowds can make otherwise perfectly sane people do otherwise inexplicable things: run down the road with traffic cones on their heads, applaud at the end of Justin Bieber concerts, and as we now know, herd others into gas chambers and onto killing fields.

Demagoguery is, of course, the bane of politics; but it is also much to be feared in the church. I have often mentioned my dislike of the American evangelical tendency to exalt the great conference speaker and to allow him to do the thinking; such is surely the kind of secularization that Paul fears has invaded the church in Corinth, where crowd-pleasing aesthetics trump critical thinking. The danger in the church, therefore, is not that perfectly ordinary and decent people will construct gas chambers and usher their neighbors off to them; rather, it is the surrender of their God-given intellects to those who use the clichés, the idioms, and the buzzwords of the wider culture to herd them along a path that the leader chooses. Fear of the leader, fear of the pack, fear of not belonging, can make people do strange things.

Even more significant for Christians today, I suspect, are the peddlers of authenticity that now swarm around the web. They are easy enough to spot: the slightly out-of-focus web page photo, with eyes averted from the camera, serious, pensive expression, soul patch, glasses in a style first sported in the seventies by existentialist

11

Swedish hairdressers called Sven, perhaps torn jeans, autumnal lighting, maybe a few leaves scattered on the ground. And, above all, constant, grating references to "authenticity." Given the clichéd manner in which it is relentlessly expressed, such "authenticity" is, it seems, a somewhat synthetic product: whatever individuality the blogmeister might otherwise possess is often simply obliterated by the mass-produced idiomatic pseudo-cool of the cutting-edge crowd through which "authenticity" is expressed. It's a crowd-pleasing product that, surprise surprise, too often merely reflects the predilections of the crowd. Of course, not a few of these kinds of authentocrats quote Kierkegaard. A supreme ironist himself, SK would no doubt have appreciated the irony of Kierkegaard chic in the crowd of untruth and the fact that claims to authenticity are always in this present age sure signs that one is dealing with a phony. And yes, before anyone shouts "Physician, heal thyself!" he would probably also have been amused, in a horrified sort of way, by the irony of appearing on a mug, a commodity for the mass consumer market.

Of course, the peddlers of mass-produced authenticity are soft targets, as easy to spot as their navelocentric web musings and pictures are easy to mock. But the crowd mentality also poses a problem for the Protestant Christian without the soul patch, Sven glasses, and camera with blurred vision. The Reformed world has its dark suits, its hall of fame, and its clichéd patois of pieties as well. We may talk about truth rather than authenticity—and rightly so—but when belief in that truth becomes merely a function of being part of the crowd, then we too have failed to be truthful individuals.

There is a real tension here. Our faith demands only one mediator, and we as individuals are to put our trust in him; but we are also part of a corporate, communal entity; this communal dimension of Christianity finds expression in a common authority, that of the Bible, and a common language—that of the creeds, of the confessions, and indeed of our own distinctive traditions, by which we communicate with each other and by which we express our corporate identity. Thus we are caught always between the need to trust directly in Christ as individuals, while giving due weight to our identity as part of the larger body. The question to ask is: Is this a tension we live with as we should, or is it one that is too often resolved on one side or the other? Given the current reaction in Christian circles against individualism variously defined, and a renewed emphasis on community, it is worth asking whether the tension is not in danger of resolution in favor of the corporate and at the expense of the individual.

Take, for example, our faith. How much do we truly believe for ourselves and how much do we believe because some great figure, some leader in our chosen community, believes? Or because we just happen to belong to a church where everybody believes the same? In the American world of celebrity cults and megachurches, even in the Reformed world, this is an acutely pointed and relevant question. Indeed, one does not have to be in a megachurch to see the temptation to sit back and just belong through the formalities of public worship and the vicarious belief of the church as body. But if you take a man and put him on a desert island, or in a place where nobody believes the same things, what will happen to his faith? Will it survive? Was it more than a mere public performance or a function of belonging to a particular community? Stripped of its context, it will stand naked, and appear as it really is. To put it in a way of which Luther would have approved, only the one who has truly come to the point of despair in himself as an individual can then truly come to faith in the savior; for he cannot have another to believe on his behalf; the truth he sees is not something "out there" or reported to him by another; it necessarily involves his very being and identity. One must first believe as an individual before one can belong to the community.

This is the problem of American Christendom. Now, all of the palaver about the "end of Christendom" should not fool us into thinking that a form of Christendom does not still exist. Anywhere that Christianity has become a formality, there is Christendom; anywhere that the belief of the group substitutes for the belief of the individual, there is Christendom; anywhere the rules of the outward game can be learned, executed with panache, and substituted for the attitude of the heart, there is Christendom. And, lest we forget, the form of that formality can be orthodoxy, just as easily as it can be heterodoxy; it can be rooted in the Westminster Standards just as easily as in the tweets of the latest aspiring authentocrat; it can be found in traditional worship styles as much as in the spontaneity of the new. And, ironically, American individualism feeds directly into this negation of the individual: the individual as consumer, as dilettante, thrives in a world of large, anonymous churches, churches that happily continue week by week with only 10 percent of the people engaged in giving of time and money; there are no demands made on the 90 percent of individuals who make up the corporate entity precisely because the body is essentially self-perpetuating. The crowd is truly untruth at that point.

This tension in orthodox Christianity, between being necessarily part of a whole and an individual accountable to God, is something with which all Christians must wrestle. To resolve it one way or the other would be to lose something crucial, for the Christian faith demands we reject both solipsistic piety and also any notion of the crowd as our mediator. The one cuts us off from the body; the other makes us mere passengers who never engage God for ourselves.

There are no easy answers to this; that's what makes it such an interesting and irresolvable tension. But, as it stands, the church in America seems to have the worst of both worlds: an individualism that does not lead to true individual existence as a Christian, one where I truly take responsibility for myself before God, but one where I allow others to do it for me; and that therefore plunges inexorably toward the anonymity of the mega-church and the laziness of the pew-sitting Sunday passenger.

It is not simply the crowd that is untruth at that point. It is the church as well.

One of the amazing things about modern American culture is surely the pathological fear of wasting time. It is especially evident in the attitude toward children. Public school kids have their lives scheduled from morning till night; homeschool parents seem to regard any second of the day from the age of two that isn't used to learn Latin poetry or the cello or conversational Swahili as time that is wasted. It's a far cry from my childhood, when school ran from 9 in the morning till 4 in the afternoon, and then I was free to ride my bike, walk on the common, or just sit around with friends. And it continues into later life: all the technology we have, and people seem to have less free time than ever.

Indeed, we have surely lost the virtue that is laziness. As Kierkegaard once said, "Far from idleness being the root of all evil, it is rather the only true good"—a truly amazing theological insight. Some may think that may be going a bit far, but compared with the idea that the essence of humanity is busy-ness, it is much to be preferred.

The greatest testament to the power of wasted time in the history of the church is surely Luther's *Table Talk*. A collection of anecdotes and sayings collected by Luther's closest friends, it reflects the full range of Luther as pastor, mentor, Christian, and friend. Reading the comments, from advice to young preachers ("The sixth mark of a good preacher is knowing when to stop") to comments on lawyers ("One only studies something as dirty as law in order to make money") to general observations on life, some of which don't bear repeating on a polite blog such as this. I suspect Luther's table companions learned more about life and ministry while drinking beer and having a laugh with the Meister than in the university lecture hall.

Numerous applications come to mind: seminary is the people with whom you strike up friendships (a point that must be taken into account as seminaries move toward more distance education); friendships (real, embodied friendships that are not exclusively mediated through pixels) are crucial to staying the course of ministry—laughter in the face of adversity and hardship not only being vital in this regard but also, of course, an almost exclusively social phenomenon that requires company; drinking beer with friends is perhaps the most underestimated of all Reformation insights and essential to ongoing reform; and wasting time with a choice friend or two on a regular basis might be the best investment of time you ever make.

3

Messiahs Pointed
to the Door

March 2009

THERE ARE MANY DIFFERENCES between
American and British culture. Most obvious, perhaps, are the
sports: baseball versus cricket; and football (where feet are rarely
used) versus football (where feet, and the occasional head, are all
that can be used); and even, once again, football (where pads are
compulsory and no period of action lasts for more than five seconds) versus rugby (where pads are the despised accouterments
of pansies and where, unless you can actually run for more than
five seconds, you are likely to get flattened). The list of American
idiosyncrasies could go on: the American penchant for men's
shoes with tassels (which, I am thankful, have no counterpart in
Britain); the post-colonial idea that a sausage on a lollipop stick
is edible; and the constitutional right to eat cheese delivered
from an aerosol can without government interference. Freedom
is surely a wonderful thing.

Joking aside, there is one other aspect of American culture that is perhaps most obvious at this particular moment in time: the cult of the individual celebrity. Now, "celebs" and the vacuous hoo-hah that surrounds them seem to be a cultural universal, one that scarcely distinguishes America from Britain; but a closer examination reveals that there are significant differences that are instructive between the way celebrity functions in the two cultures.

Take sport, for example. What is most striking to a British expat about American sports is the focus on the individual superstar. In Britain, by and large, team sports focus on the team; rarely does the team become merely an adjunct to the individual. Two exceptions in the world of football come to mind: Georgie Best in the late 1960s and 1970s and David Beckham in the 1990s and continuing to the present. These men did develop something akin to cult followings; but, besides them, one is hard-pressed to think of any others who ever emerged from the sport in a way that made them bigger than the teams for which they played, or made them the focal point or fundamental identity mark of a team. The same is even more true in rugby: I support Gloucester and England with a passion; but my focus is always on the whole, not any of the individual parts. Players come, players go; I'm hard-pressed to remember names from the team three years ago. None rises to the level of celebrity that makes them the essence of the team at any given point.

American sport is very different. In Philadelphia, football is all about Donovan McNabb, and the fortunes of the team are intimately connected to him as a person. When the Eagles play the Cowboys, yes, it is Eagles versus Cowboys but, even more so, it is

McNabb versus his old teammate and now rival, Terrell Owens. This is replicated across sports: Michael Jordan, Magic Johnson, Shaq, AI, A-Rod, etc, etc. The cult of the individual personality, as opposed to the cult of the institution, seems deeply ingrained in the American sporting world.

The same is true in politics. It has been fascinating over recent months listening to the rhetoric surrounding the election of President Obama. It reminded me of nothing so much as the Labour Party election victory in Britain in 1997. For those too young to remember, Britain had elected a Conservative government since 1979—from '79 to '90 under Mrs. Thatcher, then from '90 to '97 under John Major. When Tony Blair's Labour Party swept the Tories away, it ended nearly two decades of Tory political domination, and of Labour's internal disarray. Of course, eighteen years in power had made the Tories into a corrupt and complacent political gang, and the popular sigh of relief that they had finally been shown the door was palpable. People talked on the news about a new dawn, about a feeling of hope across the nation, about a fresh start, about the potential for a bright new future. Of course, "new" Labour soon showed themselves to be as sleazy and corrupt as the "old" Tories, but that's not my point: the point is that the language of hope and expectation was focused on an institution, the Labour Party, rather than on Tony Blair as an individual.

The election of Obama has generated similar rhetoric in the U.S. Like the Labour Party, he replaces a morally discredited and deeply unpopular executive; people want a change from the old ways of doing things; Obama is likable and articulate; it is inevitable that he is receiving much good press and popular acclaim in his early days in office; and, like the Labour Party, it is certain that he will disappoint on many fronts. What is different from Britain in 1997, however, is that the rhetoric of hope is focused on him as an individual rather than on the Democratic Party as an institution. He may not be a king, but the language used about him would seem to indicate he, as an individual, is regarded as embodying the nation, as carrying the nation's hopes, as the one with whom we will all stand or fall, and as the one who will be able to deliver. American presidential elections are ultimately, and inevitably, about individual personalities; that is not the case in Britain: have you ever wondered why Winston Churchill lost the 1945 General Election between V-E Day and V-J Day, the moment of his greatest personal triumph?

Numerous thoughts come to mind at this point. First, the Obama rhetoric, like the "W" rhetoric before it, is quintessentially American. A nation built on the frontier, on wide open spaces, on the rugged individual forging ahead against the odds, is still apparently wedded to the Great Man Theory of history. But history does not work like that. As any student who has managed to stay awake during any of my classes at Westminster would tell you: social and economic conditions apply. No man is great enough to single-handedly change the great social and economic forces that drive history along. It is simply absurd to think that an individual, be it George W. Bush or Barack Obama, can make that much difference. That is not how history works: to repeat, social and economic conditions still apply, even in a nation that believes all you need is the political equivalent of John Wayne or Clint Eastwood to run the problems—moral, economic, social—out of Dodge. Obama is doomed to fail on at least some of the things that are being expected from him because he stands under, not above, these macro-historical forces. This should be a sobering thought for his supporters and an encouraging thought for his detractors: the former should make their expectations of his positive contribution more realistic; the latter should not overestimate the damage he can do.

Second, this should make us sit up and think about the power of politics and particularly individual politicians. To invest so much in an individual betrays a profoundly Pelagian understanding of reality. As new Labour ultimately proved more corrupt (and arrived in Sleazeville more quickly) than the Thatcher-Major governments, so Obama is a fallen man, surrounded by fallen men and women. We should not expect too much from them: politics is messy and dirty at the best of times; the best we can hope for is that they might prove less messy and dirty than some of their predecessors.

Third, as well as being Pelagian, the rhetoric of American politics is too often Manichean: a battle between good and evil, with clear moral monopolies being attributed to different sides by their various supporters and detractors. Rush Limbaugh and Keith Olbermann are great examples of Manichean thinkers, albeit with very unmanichean senses of humor. Would that life were as simple as these men make it out to be, that political thinking and decision making were a "slam dunk" as Americans might say, or a simple "kick between the posts" to use a more British idiom; that political differences provided a simple way of reading moral differences, because the "goodies" all think one way and the "baddies" all think the other. But politics isn't simple: it's a dirty, pragmatic business that involves practical compromises left, right, and center (if there is any center remaining!). This is not to say that our laws and our policies and our platforms should not represent high aspirations; but it is to say that the reality is always somewhat more complex than ideal aspirations allow, and an acknowledgment of that fact is an important part of the political thinking and action itself.

Finally, we need to move beyond the messiah complex that is perhaps now part of the essence of the American presidential process, where so much significance is, at least at a popular cultural level, invested in one individual. Indeed, it is amazing that a country that is typically very suspicious of the government as a corporate institution is willing to put so much trust in a single person. In Britain, it is virtually the opposite: often a blind trust in institutions but a deep distrust of individual politicians.

When I listen to the hopes and aspirations of people relative to President Obama, my mind goes back not only to the '97 elections in Britain but also to The Who's great rock opera *Tommy*. Toward the end, in the song "I'm Free," Roger Daltrey sings

> But you've been told many times before
> Messiahs pointed to the door
> And no one had the guts to leave the temple!

Well, we've all been told many times before. Many political messiahs have come and gone; and, as the great British Parliamentarian Enoch Powell once commented: all political careers end in failure. Perhaps not so much in America, where presidential term limits mean that a leader cannot do the heavyweight boxing champ thing and go on too long until he gets his one-way ticket to Palookaville; but even given this, the most successful American politicians can only achieve a fraction of what they want, and inevitably make compromises and dirty their hands along the way.

And, of course, as in politics, so in religion. The American political process, as I argued above, is simply the most dramatic example of the Great Man Theory of history that pervades American society. I had often wondered why certain British figures—Jim Packer, N. T. Wright, Alister McGrath, etc., were much bigger this side of the Atlantic than back home in their native country. Was it just the accent? Surely it couldn't be the dentistry? Maybe the dress sense? No. It has all to do with the way America is a personality/celebrity-oriented culture in a way that Britain, while she may well be catching up, has historically not been. The American church reflects the culture: ministries built around individuals, around big shots; churches that focus on god-like guru figures, all of them pointing to one door. I have lost count of the conversations I have had with church people anxious to tell who they heard at this conference, which person they corresponded with, how this opinion or that opinion would not sit well with this demigod and is therefore of little value— and, of course, how anyone who disagrees with, or criticizes, this chosen hero must of necessity be morally depraved and wicked. People want the gods to do their thinking for them. All of the Pelagian/Manichean celebrity malarkey of the American political process is alive and well in the church as well. The question is: When it comes to churches and ministries built around messiahs who are supposed to point not to themselves but to the true door, who is going to have the guts to leave the temple?

I found myself in the invidious position of having to issue a clarification and apology for a theological analysis of an American "sport" (sic):

I claimed in class today that basketball was not only the quintessential American game but also the quintessential Pelagian game. My evidence was that every time you get the ball, you score, so it's all about quantity, not quality (hence American), and everybody gets to feel pretty good about themselves (hence Pelagian). I stand corrected: a student pointed out that, very occasionally, a team may get the ball and not score. Thus, basketball is, I guess, a semi-Pelagian game and not quite as bad as I had argued.

Apologies for any offense.

4

THE NAMELESS ONE

September 2009

OVER THE LAST FEW MONTHS, I have been asked in numerous contexts what I think about the Young, Restless, Reformed (YRR) movement(s) described in Collin Hansen's book of the same name. I did do a quasi-review of this book some time ago, in which I argued that the existence of the movement seemed to indicate that all the hype surrounding the Emergent business was probably overwrought, and that there was no need for complete panic in Reformed circles.

In retrospect, however, there are a number of things that should give some cause for critical reflection on this new interest in Reformed theology. Let me preface this by saying that the more people reading the Bible, the better, as far as I am concerned; the more people going to church and hearing the gospel preached, the more we should all be rejoicing; and the more people studying the writings of Calvin, Owen, and company, the happier we should all be. Only the modern-day equivalents of the Scottish

Moderates of the eighteenth and nineteenth centuries would grumble and complain that more people are spending more time hearing more sermons, reading more Scripture, and studying more classic Christian literature. But just because a movement has good effects does not mean that we should be blind to its shortcomings and potential pitfalls.

One striking and worrying aspect of the movement is how personality oriented it is. It is identified with certain big names rather than creeds, confessions, denominations, or even local congregations. Such has always been the way with Christianity to some extent. Luther was a hero, both in his own time and for subsequent generations, and he is hardly alone. The names of Owen, Edwards, and Spurgeon, to list but three, also have great cachet; and, if we are honest, there are things we all find in their writing that are scarcely unique to them but that we are inclined to take more seriously because it is these men who wrote the words on the page.

Yet the hype surrounding today's leaders of the YRR movement far outstrips anything these earlier heroes enjoyed in their lifetimes; indeed, Luther never became rich, despite his great stature, and never headed up a ministry named after himself, or posted a fee schedule for speaking engagements on his website. Far from it. He even had to take employment as a gardener and a carpenter to make ends meet during the Reformation; and neither Owen, Edwards, nor Spurgeon ever enjoyed the good life to any great extent, with the latter even having his life arguably shortened by the battle for truth in which he engaged firsthand, not via the comfort of a conference stage or a podcast. The significance of the leaders of the YRR movement, however, seems less like that of ages past and at times more akin to the broader cultural phenomenon of the modern cult of celebrity, a kind of sanctified Christian equivalent of the secular values that surround us. The world has Brad, Angelina, Tom, Barack, and so on; the Christian world has—well, I am sure the reader is quite capable of filling in the blanks. All too often we're a bit too much like the church in Corinth, with its Christian competitive equivalents to pagan Sophists.

Idolatry à la 1 Corinthians 1 is not the only danger, of course. Often cults of personality can degenerate in short order into cults, pure and simple, especially when every word of the guru figure becomes virtual Holy Writ among the gnostic initiates. At a relatively harmless level, we can see the fruit of this cultic leader-follower dynamic in the predictably irrational and excessive language used by the disciples of men like N. T. Wright concerning those who criticize the Great Leader; but pseudonymous wacko bloggers are one thing, actual church community structures are quite another; and history is littered with the serious human wreckage caused when good Christian people start worshiping the messenger rather than the One to whom the message refers. A cultic devotion to a leader, combined with the kind of authority structures that churches necessarily have in order to function as churches, can prove a sometimes deadly and always painful mix.

The supply-side economics of the YRR movement is also worrying here, as it can easily foster such idolatry by building up a leader's importance out of all proportion to his talent. Let's face it: no preacher is so good that his every sermon deserves to be printed or his every thought published; but some contemporary leaders are heading fast in that direction, and this can only fuel their cultic significance for those needing someone to follow. Come on, chaps, everyone preaches a disastrous clunker once in a while; many actually preach them with remarkable and impressive regularity. The world therefore does not need to read every word you ever utter from a pulpit; and not every electrical impulse that sparks between the synapses in your gray matter needs to be written down, turned into yet another expository commentary, and sold for 15 percent net royalties at the local Christian bookshop.

If leader-as-celebrity-and-oracular-source-of-all-knowledge is one potential problem in the YRR culture, then another concern is the apparent non-exportability of the models of church on offer. Everyone knows the amazing works that have been done through the ministries of men such as Tim Keller in Manhattan and Mark Driscoll in Seattle; but the track record of exporting the Redeemer or Mars Hill models elsewhere is patchy at best, raising the obvious question of whether these phenomena are the result less of their general validity and more of the singular talents of the remarkable individuals. To be clear, this is in no way to suggest that these churches are not faithful; it is to ask whether they are not more rare and unrepeatable than is often acknowledged. If the secret lies in the gifts of the individual leader, then time spent trying to replicate the models elsewhere with less-talented or differently gifted leaders is doomed to failure and a waste of time.

We have been here before. I spent my early Christian years among people always looking for the "new Lloyd-Jones," or preaching for an hour when they only had thirty minutes of material to present. So guess what? The reincarnate Lloyd-Jones never came, and too many English evangelical congregations resigned themselves to thirty minutes of quality negated by thirty minutes of agony every Sunday. We wasted time and valuable talent in trying to impersonate him or to identify the next one of his ilk to come along.

Carrying on from this danger of personality cults, part of me also wonders whether the excitement surrounding the movement is generated because people see that Reformed theology has intrinsic truth, or because they see that it works, at least along the typical American lines of numbers of bodies on seats (in Britain, we'd say "bums on seats" but that phrase rather gains in translation). Now, I am no member of the theological party that sees the Lord's blessing in the fact that every year its churches are smaller, its sermons more arcane, self-important, and tedious, and its people less friendly and more sour. Look, if I wanted a pretentious and incomprehensibly abstract theology with an impeccable record of emptying churches, I'd convert to Barthianism, wouldn't I? Yet not reveling in smallness and irrelevance does not require that I necessarily regard increasing numerical and financial size as accurate gauges of fidelity and truth.

Much has rightly been made by Reformed people of the problem of an understanding of Christianity that is driven by pragmatism, as exemplified by the Joel Osteen "be a Christian and be a better you" mentality; much criticism has also been lodged against the church-growth movement because of its tendency (in the words of an old song) to find out what they like, and how they like it, and let them have it just that way. But the dangerous thing about pragmatism is that it does not necessarily reject the truth; it merely renders it subordinate to the desired end. To be precise, pragmatism evaluates means in terms of impact and results; and the implication of this is that even means that are intrinsically true can still be co-opted by pragmatism simply because they seem to be achieving the desired results at some particular point in time. Now the gospel has always been true, in the good years and the lean; and we need to be certain that the current enthusiasm for Reformed theology is rooted in an acknowledgment of its intrinsic truth, and not simply in the fact that, at this point in time, Calvinism is cool enough to pull in the punters.

Finally, I worry that a movement built on megachurches, mega-conferences, and megaleaders does the church a disservice in one very important way that is often missed amid all the pizzazz and excitement: it creates the idea that church life is always going to be big, loud, and exhilarating, and thus gives church members and ministerial candidates unrealistic expectations of the normal Christian life. In the real world, many, perhaps most, of us worship and work in churches of a hundred people or fewer; life is not loud and exciting; big things do not happen every Sunday; budgets are incredibly tight and barely provide enough for a pastor's modest salary; each Lord's Day we go through the same routines of worship services, of hearing the gospel proclaimed, of taking the Lord's Supper, of teaching Sunday School; perhaps several times a year we do leaflet drops in the neighborhood with very few results; at Christmastime we carol sing in the high street and hand out invitations to church, and maybe two or three people actually come along as a result; but no matter—we keep going, giving, and praying as we can; we try to be faithful in the little entrusted to us. It's boring, it's routine, and it's the same, year in, year out. Therefore, in a world where excitement, celebrity, and cultural power are the ideal, it is tempting amid the circumstances of ordinary church life to forget that this, the routine of the ordinary, the boring, the plodding, is actually the norm for church life and has been so throughout most places for most of the history of the church; that mega-whatevers are the exception, not the rule; and that the church has survived throughout the ages not just—or even primarily—because of the high-profile fireworks displays of the great and the good, but because of the day-to-day faithfulness of the mundane, anonymous, nondescript people who constitute most of the church, and who do the grunt work and the tedious jobs that need to be done. History does not generally record their names, but the likelihood is that you worship in a church that owes everything, humanly speaking, to such people.

Ultimately, only the long term will show whether the YRR movement has genuinely orthodox backbone and stamina, whether it is inextricably and inseparably linked to uniquely talented leaders, and whether "Calvinism is cool" is just one more sales pitch in the religious section of the cultural department store. If the movement is more marketing than reality, then ten to fifteen years should allow us to tell. If it is still orthodox by that point, we can be reasonably sure it is genuine. Indeed, when torn jeans, or nose rings, or ministers talking about their sex lives from the pulpit become passé or so commonplace that they cease to be distinctive, we will see whether it is timeless truth or marketable trendiness that has really driven the movement; and, even it proves to have been the latter, we should not panic. We will still be left with the boring, mundane, and nameless people and culturally irrelevant and marginal churches—the nameless ones—upon whose anonymous contributions, past and present, most of us actually depend.

I was talking with someone last week about a well-known theological personality. "I don't think he wants to be a heretic" was my friend's comment. "No," I responded, "I think the problem is he wants to be a big shot." It reminded me of the reflections of another friend on a New Testament passage that I cited in a recent e-mail exchange with Martin Downes—1 Timothy 1:5–7 (here I use the ESV):

> The aim of our charge is love that issues from a pure heart and a good conscience and a sincere faith. Certain persons, by swerving from these, have wandered away into vain discussion, desiring to be teachers of the law, without understanding either what they are saying or the things about which they make confident assertions.

My friend made two observations about this passage. First, the drift into dubious theological discussion is here described as moral in origin: these characters have swerved from a pure heart, a good conscience, and a sincere faith; that is why their theology is so dreadful. Second, their desire is not to teach but to be teachers. There is an important difference here: their focus is on their own status, not on the words they proclaim. At most, the latter are merely instrumental to getting them status and boosting their careers.

Thus, what concerns me most is that students may simply desire to be teachers. If that is their motivation, then they have already abandoned a pure heart, a good conscience, and a sincere faith, and their theology, no matter how orthodox, is just a means to an end and no sound thing. It is why I am very skeptical of the internal call to the ministry as a decisive or motivating factor in seeking ordination. Nine times out of ten, I believe that the church should first discern who should be considering the Christian ministry, not simply act as a rubber stamp for a putative internal call that an individual may think he has.

Further, such students whose first desire is to be teachers are more likely to try to catch whatever is the latest trendy wave. Orthodoxy is always doomed to seem uncreative and pedestrian in the wider arena; if the aim is to be a teacher, to be the big shot, then it is more likely that orthodoxy will be less appealing in the long run—although there are those for whom orthodoxy, too, is simply a means to being a celebrity.

In this sense, orthodoxy can be heresy as well.

5

Pro-Choice Not Pro-Options

December 2009

RECENTLY, A FRIEND quoted John Kennedy to me: "To lead is to choose." This quotation is not one that I have been able to verify, but whether Kennedy said it or not, it is surely a piece of brilliant insight on the nature of leadership. One of the luxuries of having no power or influence is surely the fact that one never has to make any significant choices. Sure, one can choose to support this leader or that leader, to argue for this side or that side of an issue; but because such support and such arguments are hypothetical and insignificant, because the responsibility for the decision or the policy lies in the hands of somebody else, then if it all goes horribly wrong, one always has the option of walking away while telling onlookers, "It was nothing to do with me." The leader has no such luxury: ultimately, he not only has to support one side of an argument but he has to act consistent with that; once he does so, his ability to walk away unscathed if it all goes down the drain is reduced to zero.

The "Kennedy quotation" reminded me of another comment from Washington, not this time from a politician but from Mark Dever, pastor of Capitol Hill Baptist Church. Several times over the years I have heard Mark fulminate against what he sees as the "cult of options" that is so important for young people today. In essence, the cult of options is the desire to keep all life options open, of not making commitments that close down possibilities in the future. Arguably, this is a function of a consumer society where choice is exalted as a virtue; it is perhaps particularly ingrained in America where even the education system allows for options to be kept open even to university level. In Britain, at least in my day, you limited your academic subjects to three at the age of sixteen, and thus the fundamental choice—arts or sciences—was made very early on. Against this cult of options, Mark argues strongly for committing oneself early to particular things and thus cutting off the temptation to choose and to drift and to drift and to choose throughout life.

Combining the thought of Kennedy and that of Mark, however, raises a key question: If it is true that this generation is addicted to the cult of choice and of keeping all options open, is it not the case that this generation is ill-equipped to hold any position of leadership? If part of the essence of leadership is to choose, to decide, to commit to a course of action or a policy, and thereby close off other possibilities, then surely those who are incapable or unwilling to do so are likely to prove disastrous in positions of leadership?

Certainly, much of the culture surrounding Christianity at the moment militates against the kind of commitment that making a choice, rather than merely having a choice, demands. The language of conversation, so popular in certain quarters, has a certain open-ended quality to it. Once upon a time, arguments and debates were designed for the express purpose of reaching a conclusion, of deciding which, if any, of two or more positions was the best or the strongest or the most true. Conversation has more of an "I'll hear what you say, you hear what I say, and we can all agree to differ while remaining friends" feel.

This perhaps connects to what is now generally recognized as the extended adolescence of many young people today. In the U.K., a journalist recently lamented the increasingly common habit of middle-aged men walking round with their jeans halfway down their backsides, showing off their designer underwear in imitation of their teenage sons. In my day, the only middle-aged men who did so were workers on building sites, and they generally were not sporting Calvin Klein boxers but rather revealing too much pallid flesh and cleavage. Nowadays, any emotionally stunted thirty-something apparently feels free so to do and thinks it makes him cool, although what his teenage kids might think about the significance of Dad's sartorial style is another matter. My own kids cringe when I sport my T-shirt from a recent Who concert; if I walked round showing off my tighty whities, they would die of embarrassment.

Of course, there are many other aspects of our culture that point to this reality of emotional retardation. The compulsive need of some to be liked, to the extent that any criticism of them generates visceral and personal responses, speaks of a deeply insecure and immature section in our culture. Then I scarcely need to mention the amount of buck-passing and refusal to take responsibility that goes on, where every stupid action someone performs can always be laid at the feet of somebody else. Scald yourself with hot coffee? Sue the guy who made the kettle. Can't seem to get that promotion at work? Must have been because your daddy didn't tell you he loved you often enough. Cheat on your wife? Well, the missus should have been more understanding and then you wouldn't have gone looking elsewhere.

All of this is sad in a tragicomical way; and it is perhaps not surprising that as adolescence creeps into middle age, so does the fear of making choices and closing down options; but I wonder whether most lethal of all will prove to be not the lack of commitment and stability that characterizes Mark's "cult of options." Rather, the worst of it may well be that a generation is growing up that is happy to sneer and snipe at the decisions of others, but for whom making decisions that bind is something they themselves are incapable of doing, an alien concept no less; and that means not only, as I suspect Mark Dever fears, that a generation will grow up with no real commitments other than to themselves as individuals, but also with no real leadership potential.

One of the striking things about great leaders in history is the strong passions they have aroused. Churchill is surely a great hero to many on both sides of the Atlantic, but, interestingly enough, my grandfather hated him with a passion because in the 1920s he had set the troops on striking miners. Lloyd George was the other great war leader Britain produced in the twentieth century, a brilliant orator and political strategist, but he was hated and reviled as much as he was praised and adored. The same is true in America: think of a significant leader in any sphere and you find someone who polarizes opinion, whether it is Franklin D. Roosevelt, General Douglas MacArthur, or Martin Luther

King Jr. Why? Because great leaders make tough choices and, in so doing, commit themselves to courses of action that can bring praise but also excoriation. They do not sit on the fence; they do not sit on the sidelines, taking potshots at those who have to make the decisions; they do not enjoy the luxury of always knowing what should be done but never actually having to take responsibility for doing it. And they understand that, sometimes, it is better to make a decision that proves to be wrong than to make no decision at all.

In short, it should be a matter of concern that we live in a world where the very values that seem increasingly to dominate our society—extended adolescence and the love of choice combined with the dislike of the responsibility of making choices—are those that will erode the very qualities that make good leaders: maturity and a willingness to make the hard decisions.

This leads to one other concern about future leadership. It is what I call the emergence of the professional statesman. The professional statesman is the person who thinks and acts as if he or she can rise above the fray and speak to issues in a way that transcends the typical struggles involved in any leadership situation. I have witnessed this so often over the last few years, both in observing the wider political scene and in the church, which seems to me to be increasingly marked by such men: they are those who try to defuse theological conflict by playing the moral equivalence card whereby they argue that the struggle is really petty and personal, a moral conflict between lesser men above which they and they alone can stand and see the way forward. My suspicion is that too often this simply reflects the problematic patterns in wider society: a need to be liked; a need to avoid making divisive decisions; and a desire to have the perks of leadership with none of the responsibilities and pain involved.

The problem is that statesmen are made, not born. They earn the right to be statesmen by fighting the battles and leading from the front. Love him or hate him, only Nixon could go to China, because only Nixon had the track record of tough-mindedness with regard to Communism that meant he could make the trip. Only Mandela could dismantle apartheid and promote reconciliation in South Africa because only he had taken the stand and paid the price that gave him the moral authority necessary. Too often I suspect that aspiring statesmen in the church are driven more by a need to be liked and to avoid conflict than by a real desire to provide strong leadership; but being a statesman is not a career path; it is something that is earned over many years of making hard decisions, taking unpopular stands, and proving one's mettle under fire. Those who simply arrive on the scene as ready-made statesmen, so to speak, or who have statesman status thrust upon them by others before they have ever had to take a tough position on anything—well, such leaders want to have their cake and eat it too: they want influence and respect, but they do not particularly want to earn it.

I often joke that my motto as academic dean at Westminster is this: "The man who has no enemies has no honor." Certainly, I suspect that any dean who is universally liked is probably not doing his job properly or enjoys a faculty that have somehow been spared the curse of original sin. But the motto could be broadened: "The leader who has no enemies has no honor." For such a leader has surely never done that which is essential to leadership—made a choice.

6

THE FREUDOM OF
THE CHRISTIAN

January 2007

CHRISTIANS OFTEN strike me as the most Freudian of people. Say what you like, I have a sneaking suspicion that Freud, rather than Augustine, Luther, or Calvin, probably offers the best insights about the way Christians really think and act.

Let me explain with some examples. The other day I was sitting in the office of a colleague, just shooting the breeze, when he pointed to a recent scholarly study of the history of eschatology and asked my opinion. "Well, Mike," I responded, "it's a great piece of scholarship, and very deeply Freudian." The two of us looked at each other and then he simply burst out laughing. "It's really all about killing the Oedipal father," I continued, with mock seriousness, moving seamlessly into "criminal profiler" mode, something I learned while working in the Scholarly Crimes Unit (SCU) at the University of Nottingham (sadly, rumors that I am the inspiration for the character Chad Schwarzkopf in the American series *Law and Order: SVU* are unfounded). "The chap who wrote that book grew up in a strongly dispensationalist-fundamentalist family; his research is, in part, a way to put all that behind him. As he demonstrates the very shaky historical foundations of dispensationalism, he is able to justify breaking away from the dogmas of his father's faith. The scholar destroys his father's theology. Oedipus kills his father. Freud had it all nailed down, didn't he?" There was a moment of silence, and then we both burst out laughing.

For what it's worth, I don't exempt myself from such psychobabbling analysis. My parents are not professing believers, and, as a result of the rebellion against their authority that my conversion represents, I suspect I have partly spent my life trying to be the kind of Christian my father could respect: an educated Christian, one with initials after his name, a fancy title, a nice office, a twisted sense of humor, a stable and happy family, a steady job, etc., etc.

Of course, life is more complicated than the analysis offered in either of the above examples; all actions and agendas are driven by a variety of factors; but I would argue that there is some significant truth in both cases. Human motivation is a profoundly complex thing, and to rule out psychological aspects at the outset seems to be a highly contentious move. Indeed, I would extrapolate and say that some of the least-attractive aspects of the modern Reformed world in particular can be fruitfully studied from the perspective of Oedipal rebellion against parents.

Take, for example, the trend in some Reformed quarters to drop the F-word and other obscenities and profanities in casual conversation. Now, I don't use the word, but I should make it clear that I am not talking here about using it in an uncontrolled moment of rage or fear in extreme circumstances; I am talking about using it in the casual way that, say, teenagers stick the word "like" into every sub-clause, or the way others of us might use "umm" or "err." Some Reformed folk, especially among the younger guys coming up through the ranks, seem to think that the use of such language in conversation is not simply permissible for the Christian but a thing greatly to be desired.

Why? Why is it that language that would offend most of my non-Christian friends, and that they would regard as a sign of seriously limited vocabulary and deep childishness, is deemed by some in the Reformed world to be, on the contrary, a sign of urbane sophistication and spiritual maturity? The answer you are likely to receive when you ask is: Christian freedom. As Christians, we are free to use such language, and doing so therefore shows what a good grasp of the gospel we really have.

I disagree. First, it is clear that New Testament teaching opposes obscene talk, so the argument is fallacious at the outset. Thus, if objecting to obscene talk is pietistic legalism, then Paul was a pietistic legalist. But even if we set that aside for the moment, it seems to me that what we are dealing with in this instance is less the matter of Christian freedom and more that of Christian Freudom: an Oedipal rebellion against older religious practices, often, although not always, those of the parents or of early Christian mentors.

As I mentioned above, I do not come from a professing Christian home, blissfully happy, loving, and stable that it was. There are certain obvious drawbacks to that; but one definite advantage is that, whatever else has screwed me up, whatever else haunts my nightmares, whatever else I am rebelling against, it is not the

Christianity of my parents. Yet so many Christians, particularly in America, seem to be driven by an overwhelming desire to slay the parental religion—if not the religion of biological parents, then often the dominant religion of previous evangelical generations. Spiritual Oedipus syndrome, a.k.a. Christian Freudom.

D. A. Carson comments in *The Gagging of God* that much of the trendy theology that characterized the neo-evangelicalism of the eighties and nineties had more than a whiff of the kind of rebellion exhibited by spoiled children whose immature self-image depends on their vocal repudiation of everything their parents held dear. What is theologically true of the trendy evangelical left seems to be practically true of the trendy Reformed right. Here, legitimate criticism of a legalistic pietism too frequently degenerates into illegitimate rubbishing of appropriate piety. Thus, the F-bomb and other casual obscenities and profanities have become, for some, the trendy hallmarks of mature Christianity. Strange to tell, talking like sexually insecure thirteen-year-olds has become the way we Christians show how grown-up we are. We embrace what the older generation rejected in order to show that we have come of age, and to show the world that, hey, we're not as weird as we used to be; we can be as rough-and-tumble, as hip, savvy, cool, and gritty as the rest.

Yet there are several problems with this. First, Christianity just isn't cool, savvy, or hip. As my sons repeatedly tell me, "Dad, you're a balding middle-aged guy; you listen to rock dinosaurs from the land that time forgot; you still call male hairdressers "barbers"; and you're a member of the Orthodox Presbyterian Church; you can never, ever be cool; and the more you try to be so, the more embarrassing you become." And the same applies to evangelical Christianity—evangelicalism just isn't cool or hip or *avant-garde*, and attempts to make it appear so, whether theologically or culturally, always end up as self-defeating, rather sad and pitiful. It doesn't matter whether you sport a ponytail, spout postmodern gobbledygook, wear a Kurt Cobain T-shirt, or have a strong opinion on which U2 album is the best—if you're an evangelical Christian, there's something ineradicably uncool about you. Anyone out there remember *The Rock Gospel Show* from the mid-eighties? I rest my case.

So is the case with Christian use of foul language: cultural historians know that obscenity is one typical cultural way to offend middle-class values; and so in the evangelical world the sight of a bunch of quintessentially comfortable middle-class white guys cussing and swearing, trying to prove that they are not, well, quintessentially comfortable middle-class white guys, is strangely reminiscent of the tabloid images of those pampered multimillionaire rap artists who sing obscenities in a pantomimic attempt to appear like cool denizens of the mean streets. If the eighties words "pseud" and "poseur" have gone out of fashion, they should be brought back immediately; they are, after all, perfect ways of describing such wannabe tough guys, whether reforming or rapping. Christian freedom? Hey, no way. Christian Freudom more like.

Yet Christian Freudom does not end with juvenile obscenity. The way that Christian freedom seems to be judged in some Reformed quarters by the ability to consume alcohol and tobacco is quite bizarre. Now, don't misunderstand me here. I enjoy cheap wine, British beer, fine brandy, and good Scotch; and I do not even regard smoking as a sin—stupid, yes; sinful, no. But to judge the vitality of one's Christian faith by the consumption of these things is as silly as to judge it by abstention. The trivial taboos of fundamentalism have become the trivial necessities of modern evangelicalism. Again, I love rock music; I love being able to listen to Dylan and Springsteen and Daltrey and Townsend without worrying that the very act of so doing is jeopardizing my soul; yet it is not at all central to my Christian identity. Thus, it is most strange that so many Reformed people see this freedom in trivial matters as that which makes them and their Christianity so superior to that of the fundamentalism of their parents' generation. I even heard of one minister who was proud that his son smoked at fourteen—as if this were some sign of biblical maturity and masculinity. If one really must judge masculinity, I would suggest that something like rock climbing or surfing or marathon running—something that involves discipline, focus, physical prowess, and skill, and the ability to handle risk and/or pain—might be somewhat more impressive than smoking a cigar. But that's beside the point: to judge Christian maturity in any way by these things is decidedly strange and quite likely to confirm many non-Christians' view of religious people as those who are emotionally stunted, immature, and obsessed with trivia.

Of course, Christian freedom is a crucial biblical doctrine, and one of the key issues that divides Protestants from Catholics. Yet to locate its primary essence in smoking a cigar while knocking back a Scotch and poking fun at some fundie bumpkin from Tennessee, or to twist it in a manner that legitimates using language that would make the teenage son of a drunken Glaswegian navvy blush for shame, seems to be a dramatic trivialization of the issue. Indeed, it is reminiscent of the way in which characters like

Hugh Hefner and Larry Flynt have become heroes of free speech. While dissidents in the Soviet Union faced years in the gulags for voicing criticism of the regime, Hefner and Flynt made millions out of pornography and yet somehow managed to become seen as martyrs to totalitarian intolerance. OK, freedom of speech is the principle for both Solzhenitsyn and for Hefner; but Hefner is simply the unfortunate collateral price you pay for the greater freedom of being able to express oneself freely on greater issues, as did Solzhenitsyn; and the real heroes of freedom are obvious to all but the most twisted. With this analogy in mind, let's not trivialize the gospel by equating spiritual maturity with silliness and swearing.

In closing, it is perhaps worth mentioning the most famous foul-mouthed Christian beer drinker of them all: Martin Luther. It is a well-known fact that his language was rough and ready, frequently obscene, and that it became more extreme and offensive the longer he lived. Over the years, scholars have wrestled with the reasons for this, from his dysfunctional relationship with his father to his chronic constipation to his desire to present himself as a man of the common people. Certainly, the extremity of his vocabulary raises all manner of interesting psychological questions. But what is interesting is that—to my knowledge—Luther does not make his foul mouth the test case of Christian freedom and maturity; and beer drinking is only the most trivial instance for him of such liberty. Indeed, Luther actually emphasizes rather different elements in his understanding of Christian freedom.

In his classic text on the doctrine, the 1520 work, *The Freedom of the Christian*, he focuses his discussion here on Christian freedom as the basis for self-sacrificial service of others.

Of course, that kind of freedom is painful. It hurts because it involves esteeming others more highly than one esteems oneself; it hurts because it involves finding freedom precisely in the setting aside of my rights and privileges to allow one to serve others; it hurts because it is analogous to the freedom Christ himself demonstrated in his own life and death—a death, incidentally, that was profoundly un-Freudian, being the result of absolute obedience and submission to his Father and of infinite mutual love between Father and Son.

This is where real Christian freedom lies: in the realization that we can do nothing to effect our own salvation; that Christ has done it all for us; and that we are therefore able to give ourselves freely and unconditionally in sacrificial service of others. The same thing, the life, death, and resurrection of Christ, is what makes it possible for me to drink beer without endangering my soul; but that is a collateral bonus of spiritual freedom and not a significant function of my spiritual maturity. It is also the same thing that motivates me not to make Christianity a laughingstock and an embarrassment through the use of foul language. Real Christian freedom is rather more to do with service of others than self-indulgence in any area of my life. The church needs more Christian freedom and much, much less Christian Freudom.

Rumor has it that Walmart, the well-known respecter of workers' rights, famous around the world for generous terms and conditions of employment, has applied to join something called the National Gay and Lesbian Chamber of Commerce. Three thoughts come to mind:

1. What on earth has anyone's sexual orientation got to do with the work of any chamber of commerce? Now, I'm just a poor street-market trader and not a high-flying corporate superstar, but the ability to make money or run a company well seems to have nothing to do with hormones.

2. Why is it that some homosexuals seem determined to replicate all of the trappings of respectable middle-class culture? Isn't the whole point of homosexuality to be avant-garde, transgressive, and rule-breaking? So why the constant need to replicate any bit of the establishment that's going? Or is there something in the very constitution of human nature that effectively contradicts itself—striving both for radical freedom and for acceptance and belonging at the same time?

3. Christians should not panic. I predict the decision will have little or no practical impact. After a typical day at work, the average employee at Walmart will have neither the time, nor the money, nor the energy to engage in any physical activity at all, let alone something unseemly.

7

Look, It's Rubbish

May 2009

A FEW YEARS AGO I was attending a conference on behalf of the seminary arranged by an organization that includes in its membership institutions from a wide variety of theological and religious perspectives. As the conference stretched over a weekend, there was a worship service arranged for the Sunday morning. I had wondered whether to attend, not knowing how such a theologically diverse group might come together in such a setting; but I finally decided to do the polite thing and show up; and, I was not disappointed. Indeed, I have been retelling the story at dinner parties ever since.

The service kicked off OK, with a short call to worship. So far so good. Then we sang a hymn. Now, I have a preference for psalms, but the hymn was fine, as far as I remember. It was then that the real fun began. The first Bible reading was from the book of Isaiah. The gentleman apologized at the outset, saying that he had been unable to obtain an inclusive-language translation of the

51

Bible, but indicated that he would make the necessary changes himself as he read the passage. I confess that, personally, I was quite relieved about that since, for one horrible second, I had imagined I was about to witness the terrifying and distressing marginalization and oppression of over half the people present. But with the necessary substitutions, I was confident that the women around me would feel suitably enfranchised and affirmed.

That's when it all started to go wrong. I do not know whether you have ever tried to "inclusivize," "unmarginalize," or "deoppressionize" on the fly, so to speak, but it is not that easy, as the gentleman was about to demonstrate in spades. Indeed, by halfway through the passage his attempts had made such an aesthetic and grammatical mess of the passage that he abandoned his laudable, liberating ambitions and returned to oppressing the women present in a really quite unacceptable fashion.

Bad as it was, that was the high point of the service. It was all downhill from then on. Next, instead of a pulpit prayer, we all had to sit and listen to a tape recording of waves crashing on a beach. This was followed by the second Scripture reading. I was thankful this one was not from the oppressive Bible translation used by the previous reader. In fact, it was not from the Bible at all but taken from a collection of poems written by African American slaves. Now, the poem was moving and thoughtfully constructed, a piece of literature; and knowing its original context gave it a certain emotional power; but it was not Scripture in any shape or form and had no obvious place within a church service.

Onward we went, and ever downward. Now came the sermon, which was a five-minute homily on the end of slavery, full of platitudes about imperialism and oppression, all of which may

have been true, and to much of which I was not actually unsympa-
thetic, but God was conspicuous only by his absence, presumably
having nothing to say about the subject at hand. Then, finally, the
pièce de résistance, the moment to which the whole service had
been leading, the climactic moment when the congregation was
taken to the very gates of heaven: the service ended, not with a
benediction or even a prayer, but with another chance to meditate,
this time not to waves crashing on a beach but to a recording of
Kenny G playing "Amazing Grace."

Words almost fail me in the narrative at this point. After all,
not being a Kenny G fan, I found myself oppressed, marginalized,
and excluded all at once. The best I can say is that it was probably
a better option than Barry Manilow singing "Copacabana."

The service was, in many ways, a multifaceted microcosm
of a lot that is wrong with the church at large today. I remember
sitting in the room and looking around at the earnest faces as
they concentrated on the crashing waves, or empathized with
the linguistic struggles of the spontaneous inclusive language
guy, or were carried heavenward by the mellifluous tone of Mr.
G's saxophone. Almost all of these people have PhDs, I thought;
many have published subtle works from distinguished academic
presses; most of them would no doubt despise me and my institution as somehow obscurantist and ignorant; and yet, when
push comes to shove, they sit here mesmerized by this garbage.
The sophisticated post-Kantian theology for which they stand
comes to this—sitting around on a Sunday morning, listening
to PC Man mangling the Bible and Kenny G playing "Amazing
Grace." I mean, give me a break. Kenny G!?! It wasn't even John
Coltrane or Charlie Parker.

Now, despite the embarrassment of scholarly riches at this service, I sat there thinking, I could not bring a non-Christian friend into this. It would be embarrassing for reasons that have nothing to do with the excess of cumulative scholarship represented; rather, for all of the doctorates in the congregation, this service would simply insult the intelligence of the typical non-Christian who, in my experience, assumes a certain correlation between the seriousness of content and the seriousness of form. Further—and ironically—I also found it hard to believe that any of us there really felt included by this liturgical mishmash: a slag heap of sub-theological fragments pulled from hither and yon into an incoherent and vacuous fiasco does not end up including everyone in general; more likely it ends up including nobody in particular. But that's liberal ecumenism for you: sophisticated on paper and in the classroom; moronic and exclusionary in practice. To coin a phrase: "Hey, it's rubbish. So let's just call it rubbish, shall we?"

The memory of this service leads me to two further reflections on the culture of theology. First, I have always been amazed at the infatuation of so many orthodox academics with their reputation in the secular universities and liberal departments. A few years back, I edited a book with Paul Helm on the doctrine of Scripture. At the time I was on faculty at the University of Aberdeen. One colleague—a friend but one of distinctly liberal leanings—referred matter-of-factly in a public lecture to the upcoming book as representing the tradition of Warfield, of which he himself did not approve; but the comment was not a sneer; rather, it was a simple statement of his impression of the book. Within a couple of days I received an e-mail from one of the contributors, asking whether this was the case and saying that, if so, he wanted to withdraw from participation. Now, it was not actually the case: the book addressed the issue of Scripture from a different direction to the concerns of Warfield; but what puzzled me—no, what disappointed me, for I understood exactly what was going on—was that this person was so terrified of being associated with Warfield. I wonder to this day whether he would have been so concerned if he had been invited to contribute to a collection of essays that someone said pointed in a Barthian or Bultmannian direction. Probably not—because those options would not be so embarrassing to mention to friends at cocktail parties in the Senior Common Room or at the next meeting of the Society of Biblical Literature.

Now I worked in secular universities long enough to know that liberal colleagues are bright enough to spot a conservative at five hundred feet. Just because you avoid contributing to certain volumes or using certain words, or because you choose to laugh when certain people to the right of you are mocked, does not win you respect from the secular academy. It is a sad fact but, as far as biblical studies and theology go, only giving up all that is distinctive about the Christian faith will ultimately do that for you. The individual to whom I referred above no doubt liked to think he was taken seriously by mainstream colleagues, but I sat as a junior faculty in enough coffee room discussions to know the real thoughts of liberal colleagues about conservatives who try to fly under the radar. They despise them for their theology; and they despise them for the fact they try to hide or minimize it. A double whammy. Given the choice—and there is always a choice—I'd rather just be despised for being a brazen conservative with loony theology, than a duplicitous conservative with loony theology. That way one can still be of use to the church and still look in the mirror with some degree of self-respect.

But who should really be embarrassed, the liberals or the conservatives, whether Catholic, Protestant, or Orthodox? When you attend the churches of liberal colleagues, you will soon realize you have no reason to be ashamed. The embarrassment that is a liberal theological service has to be experienced to be truly believed; and almost any orthodox alternative is a better bet. After all, while I am no Eastern Orthodox, there is no comparison between a service conducted according to the hidebound, unchanged, reactionary, outdated, orthodox, creedal liturgy of St. John Chrysostom and a service involving Kenny G, a tape recording of waves, some person stating the obvious about slavery, and a befuddled chap trying to avoid oppressing women by improvising a politically correct paraphrase of the Living Bible.

This, however, brings me to my second point: ironically, not all conservative services are much better than their liberal equivalents. Now, the difference is that liberal theology should inevitably lead to liturgical nonsense in a way that orthodoxy should not. After all, orthodox theology grew out of the worship and liturgy of the ancient church, so it should be no surprise that the collapse of that theology connects to the collapse of worship and liturgy. After all, it is hard to see the musical genius of Kenny G giving birth to the Nicene Creed, or, for that matter, providing an atmosphere in which the same might be sustained. When theology is, after all, merely the projection of human aspirations, church services become merely a collage of human artifacts (although the thought that Kenny G is a projection of humanity's deepest psychological aspirations is too worrying to contemplate for any length of time). When God is mere man (or woman, or both) writ large, transcendence vanishes and triviality can only be resisted by an immense act of the will.

What are surprising, therefore, are accounts of services where the theology is supposedly orthodox but the content is sheer trivia. If God is awesome, sovereign, and holy; if human beings are small, sinful, and lost; if Christ died and rose again by a most miraculous and costly act of grace, then this should impact the way things happen in church. This is not to argue for a one-size-fits-all-my-way-or-the-highway approach to church. Context and culture are important; but what is expressed through the idioms of particular cultural manifestations of the church should be awe, reverence, and, above all seriousness—not a colorless and cold miserable seriousness but a fitting amazement at the greatness of God and his grace.

A church service involving clowns or fancy dress or skits or stand-up comedy does not reflect the seriousness of the gospel; and those who take the gospel seriously should know better. Frankly, it is more appropriate to liberal theology that does not take seriously the gospel, or the God of the gospel. Serious things demand serious idioms. I heard recently of a church service involving dressing up in costume and music taken from a Tom Cruise movie. Now, if I go for my annual prostate examination, and the doctor comes into the consulting room dressed as Coco the Clown, with "Take My Breath Away" from *Top Gun* playing in the background, guess what? I'm going to take the doctor out with a left hook, flee the procedure, and probably file a complaint with the appropriate professional body. This is serious business; and if he looks like a twit and acts like a twit, then I can only conclude that he is a twit.

You can tell a lot about people's theology from what they do in church. Involve Kenny G's music in your worship service, and I can tell not only that you have no taste in music but also that you have nothing to offer theologically to those who come through the church doors; indeed, what you do have can probably be found better elsewhere. Why certain academics hanker for the approval of the people who, when they leave the lecture theater also abandon any semblance of adulthood or intelligence, beats me. More seriously, however, why certain orthodox churches strive to look like them worries me intensely. Look, it's rubbish. So let's just call it rubbish, shall we?

Visiting Mississippi was great fun. Getting to meet "Nate-Dog" and "The Gnome" and the various other criminal Welsh-types who gather around Ref21 was a pleasure. And staying at a hotel where the guy behind the desk looked like Rod Steiger in *In the Heat of the Night* and who spoke in a strange language of which the phrase "Sears Jeans" was the only one I could understand (don't ask me why or how that came up—remember Linguistics 101: words get their meaning from how they are used in a sentence). The one disappointment: couldn't get to pay homage at the grave of Robert Johnson. Why? Because he has three graves. Now one is normal, two is impressive, but three is surely just greediness or a miracle. Perhaps good old Robert had too much talent for one body; he clearly needed three resting places. Worthy of a medieval saint, that one.

But it did make me think once again of Bono's statement that the psalms are the blues of the Bible. OK, Bono is insufferably sanctimonious, and the sunglasses? Good grief! But he's onto something here. It is, of course, well known to all but Del-Boy that Robert is supposed to have obtained his guitar skill from selling his soul to the Devil at a crossroads (although I think the earliest reference to that is from the early 1960s); but the music is surely far from devilish. The poverty in the little bit of Mississippi I saw was probably no worse than that in Philly, but it gave me a feel for how the distinctive music and language of the blues could only develop amid the agony and dispossession of the rural poor in a setting like the Deep South. And blues requires suffering—compare Johnson's recordings to, say, Eric Clapton doing the same. Clapton is a technical genius on guitar, but somehow he lacks the edge that Johnson and others such as Big Bill Broonzy and B. B. King possess.

Blues arose out of, and gave voice to, the hopes and despair of the disaffected, the poor, and the marginalized. The psalms do the same for us as Christians. It's a shame that psalm singing has been neglected by 99 percent of the church and domesticated by much of the remaining 1 percent. The greatest album never recorded is surely one of psalms sung by Robert Johnson, Robert Plant, or Nina Simone. Or all three of them. Or should that be all five of them . . . ?

8

ON MEETING JOE FRAZIER: THE MISSING ELEMENT OF MODERN THEOLOGY

April 2008

AS AN AVID BOXING FAN, as soon as I knew that I was moving to Philadelphia, I e-mailed the Smokin' Joe Frazier website to let the former heavyweight champ know of my imminent arrival. OK, it was the sad action of a soon-to-be-middle-aged man trying to fulfill a childhood fantasy. I assumed it would never happen; and, true enough, the e-mail went unanswered. But, some twelve months after arriving in the City of Brotherly Love, I was at my local YMCA when, to my utter amazement, I found myself suddenly face-to-face with Smokin' Joe himself. So, what does the sad nonentity say when suddenly in the presence of greatness, of the man who probably had the most lethal left hook of his generation?

The answer? "Yo, Joe, how ya doin'?"

No. More like "Sir, it's an honor to meet you, sir, Mr. Frazier, sir."

Faced with the awesome presence of the former world champ, I responded with stammering, barely coherent awe as I shook his hand and paid internal homage.

I was reminded of this incident last year when talking to a former student about recent developments in the understanding of Paul's theology. Not my field, of course, and thus my reading in the area is somewhat limited; but at the time I was struck by apparent similarities between some of the claims being made by these "New Perspective on Paul" academics and certain theological patterns in the seventeenth and eighteenth centuries. Then, certain reconstructions of the doctrine of justification had been advocated by men such as the Puritan Richard Baxter. What interested me was not any positive connection that could be drawn between these two movements so much as the pastoral implications of what they were saying. Both Baxter and the NPP seem to offer views of justification that, at least in the categories of classical confessional Protestantism, place a higher accent on the significance of good works than said Protestantism would normally do. In the seventeenth and eighteenth centuries, this led to a serious pastoral problem with assurance: where Baxter's theology was preached, people struggled with knowing whether they stood acquitted before God.

This was my question to the former student: Will this New Perspective stuff lead to a crisis of assurance like that caused by Baxterianism? The student's answer was emphatic and enlightening: absolutely not, because these NPP people have no concept of the holiness of God.

Now, that may well be a caricature; but it points to an important structural element of theology, especially as it connects to our mind-set and experience: only those who have an overwhelming grasp of the transcendent holiness of God will ever struggle with lack of assurance. For those who think of God as, well, pretty much like themselves, or like some other common or garden god, or simply as a projection of their own sentimentality, there is no problem with assurance. If God is not that holy, then sin isn't that awful, and I'm just not that bad. Thus, if your view of God's holiness is shaped by the standards of your own mediocrity, then you are unlikely to worry too much about whether you're going to be acceptable to him. If I had not known who Joe Frazier was that day, my approach to him would have been very different; I may even have ignored him. Only because I knew who he was and what he had done did I take him so seriously and did I treat him with awed respect.

I don't want to sound too melodramatic at this point, but I am increasingly convinced that this loss of a burning sense of God's holiness is the problem of modern theology, modern biblical scholarship, and modern church life. The loss of the sense of awe at God's holiness is the thing that separates modern liberal theology from premodern theology, and that is part of the tragedy of the modern academy.

Let's start with theology. Now, "theology" as an intellectual discipline in the modern academy today is virtually impossible to define, so fragmented has it become. The old idea of systems or *summae*, coherent summaries and syntheses of biblical teaching, has been sacrificed for a cacophony of competing subdisciplines: feminist theology; eco-theology; various ethnic theologies;

theologies of animal rights; theologies of liberation, etc., etc. In part this is an aesthetic thing: the world in which we live, dazzled by its all-consuming consumerism, loves the eclectic, the kaleidoscopic, the vibrantly chaotic. Further, the whole notion of tolerance, conceived of in a way that demands that nothing but received wisdom be given the status of an absolute, makes those traditional claims to classical theological truth seem obnoxious and oppressive—such things inhibit our social and intellectual consumerism, after all. Yet there is also a deeper reason for the loss of this disciplinary unity: the loss of a high view of the Bible as the Word of God, spoken by the one God through human authors, and thus possessing an inherent, personal, theological unity and authority. Once we have turned away from the notion of the one divine, holy author of an authoritative and ultimately unified biblical revelation, we have lost the foundation on which we can build our theology in any coherent, unified way; and that move is a profoundly profane one. Once God has, in effect, been prevented from speaking to us, we lose our ability to speak about him. Thus, this loss of a doctrine of Scripture involves the downplaying, if not the ignoring, of the voice of the awesome and holy God; and such a move can only be made when we lose sight of God himself. In other words, the persistent way in which modern theologians allow context to determine content, and the kaleidoscopic nature of human existence to drive a theology committed to an aesthetic of creative chaos, are both symbolic and constitutive of human rebellion.

It plays out similarly in the liberal academy in biblical scholarship, where too often diversity drowns unity—but it's not a problem, we're told. Of course, it's not a problem because we have bought into the random incoherence of postmodernity, judge the Bible by the standards of our own cultural expectations, and rejoice in the problem as if it were the solution. Further, the liberal Bible scholar has no problem with handling the biblical text in a casual way, as if it were just another human artifact, subject to the same profane dissection and analysis as any other piece of literature. To study the biblical text is a high calling indeed; but if you attend a classroom lecture on the biblical text, or read a book on the same, and come away without feeling awe in your heart at the amazing nature of God's gracious revelation in and through his perfect Word, then either the lecturer or author has failed to treat the text with appropriate reverence, or your heart is so hardened that you failed to sense what they were doing. We must as Christians approach the text with awe and reverence, as the words of a holy, transcendent, speaking God. To do otherwise may be scholarship in the most profane sense of the word but it is not, in the true sense of the word, biblical. After all, it clearly takes no account of the Bible's own teaching about God's terrifying holiness.

Finally, and perhaps most tragically of all, we see the loss of a sense of God's holiness in church. When prayers become the equivalent of "Yo, how you doin'?!" then something has gone awry. Public prayer should lead people into the presence of God, and that should be a humbling, if not crushing experience. When was the last time a pulpit prayer left you in awe of the God who humbles himself so that you might worship him? What about sermons? How many of us sit in judgment on the sermon, grading it for quality, length, clarity, interest, as the minister brings to us the Word of God? If we have any grasp of God's holiness, and any inkling of the importance of the prophetic task of preaching, we won't be giving the minister a grade; rather, we will be sitting and listening to what he has to say, acutely conscious of our own unworthiness to hear God as he speaks to us. Then, when the songs we sing can be summarized by the phrase "Jesus is my best boyfriend," we can be sure that something is seriously out of joint. The words we sing to God should reflect the gravity of the words God first speaks to us. Then, when church itself becomes a take-it-or-leave-it venture that we can turn up for at a time that suits us, perhaps even sipping lattes from Starbucks as we take our seats, something is seriously missing. What is it? Well, the answer isn't rocket science: a sense of the deep holiness of God. The casual nature of the postmodern world, where all hierarchies are oppressive and the consumer is king, cannot even begin to understand the void that lies at the heart of such slapdash Christianity. Your doctrine can be as correct and confessional as possible; but if it is all just so much of a game, then it is no theology at all.

Helmut Thielicke put it well when he said that God is never the object of theology, he is always the subject. In his awesome holiness, he speaks, he sets the agenda, and we are simply to respond in reverence and awe. Gregory Nazianzus said something similar in his *Theological Oration 27* where he even raised the bar to a high level for those merely listening to theological discussion, because of the holy God whose speech made such discussion possible:

> Who should listen to discussions of theology? Those for whom it is a serious undertaking, not just another subject like any other for entertaining small-talk, after the races, the theater, songs, food, and sex: for there are people who count chatter

on theology and clever deployment of arguments as one of their amusements.[1]

Theology, whether that of the high-powered scholar or the average church member, is to be shot through with holiness. The trivial way in which theology is pursued in church, but especially in the evangelical academy, is a sign that hard times are ahead. Indeed, it is a sign that the God with whom we have to do in these places is certainly not the God of the Bible. Woe to those who treat the Word of God as a light thing; woe to those who argue theology as if it were merely one more area of academic interest where scholars can disagree; woe to those whose books and articles on God or his Bible give no sense of his awesome holiness. We who aspire to be teachers and yet who tread on the holiness of God as if it were a light thing: beware, for we stand in danger of leading little ones astray, and it would be better for us if we had never been born. Pray that God grant us all an overwhelming sense of who he is.

1. St. Gregory Nazianzus, *On God and Christ*, trans. Fred Williams (Yonkers, NY: St. Vladimir's Seminary Press, 2002), 27.

9

The Freedom of the Christian Market

October 2008

SINCE ARRIVING IN THE U.S. some seven years
ago, I have become accustomed to questions asking me what it is
like to come from a socialist country. Now, I'm not sure exactly
what constitutes a "socialist" country, but in the popular American
imagination it seems to focus on the provision of a national (or
"socialized") health service. The merits and demerits of such a system are often debated on anecdotal evidence—good experiences
here, bad experiences there. Few Americans (or British people) I
have met have any real mastery of the economic arguments pro
and con, but passions run deep on both sides of the debate.

Ironically, of course, the last few weeks have seen America
become more of a socialist country than the U.K. has ever been.
After a series of catastrophic crises on the financial markets, the
federal government seems to be stepping in to bail out the banking

system. In short, one could provocatively state this in the following terms: the government is in the process of nationalizing the banks. Forget the National Health Service; when the government buys the banks, your savings, and your debts, that is socialism.

The irony is, I hope, not lost on those on the Christian Right who so closely identify biblical Christianity with the American way of free marketing. I suppose that, in the U.S., it is perhaps a little difficult to do anything else, given the fact that both of the major political parties essentially agree on the virtues of capitalism, democracy, etc. It is the air that everyone breathes, and, to be honest, there are no realistic alternatives out there; it is therefore perhaps not surprising that they have taken on the status of absolute, nonnegotiable truths, with differences appearing rather in other areas, be they identity politics, details of tax allocations, etc. Despite the Manichean, apocalyptic rhetoric that you get from both sides, the current American election is, indeed, an election about almost nothing, given that, if past records are anything to go by, a victorious Republican will likely be as socially liberal in practice as a Democrat, and a victorious Democrat as fiscally prudent (or not) as a Republican. Either way, the fundamentals of the free market will be unquestioned, since we stand at the end of a thirty-year period where its principles have reached their apotheosis, with everything from problems with healthcare to environmental pollution apparently susceptible to solution if only the markets can be freed up to do their business.

Yet the current banking crisis indicates that the system is not infallible. Of course, we have seen tremors like this before: the number of airline companies that have been on the verge of bankruptcy and kept afloat by government intervention just seems to keep on growing. They are too big to fail, or so the wisdom has it; well, if airlines are too big to fail, then for sure those companies that basically underwrite the country's mortgage debt and determine the price of money are too big to fail. Hence, the need for government bailouts.

The markets have failed, and this should (I hope!) give those Christians with a blithe faith in the free market system at least some pause for thought. Why, we should ask, has this system that is supposed to be self-regulating been so badly shaken? Who is responsible?

Now, I have studied history too long to believe that it is ultimately driven by great individuals. The Great Man Theory of history, so ably expounded by Thomas Carlyle in the nineteenth century, has a certain romantic appeal, and might still speak to the benighted followers of such as Ayn Rand, but it can scarcely account for the facts. History is shaped by much larger social, economic, and cultural forces than can ever be summed up by, focused, or determined by a single individual. The role of Hitler and Stalin as individuals was critical in the Second World War; but had they never existed, in all likelihood, the ongoing crisis in European politics that was the aftermath of the First World War would have caused some immense conflagration—Goebbels could have been a Hitler; Molotov or Mikoyan a Stalin; and it goes without saying that one lunatic with a deep-seated hatred of the Jews could not organize the Holocaust all by himself; rather, the social, cultural, and economic conditions all had to be aligned for such a thing to take place.

All of this is to say that, when we look at the crisis in the markets and try to play the blame game, then we should avoid

71

reducing the problem to one individual or even to groups. Cries of "It's the president," "It's Congress," "It's the Democrats," "It's the Republicans," and "It's the banks" all have a certain appeal. After all, it's always good to blame "them" rather than "us." Indeed, speaking for myself, I reckon it was the Welsh wot dunnit all along; and any evidence to the contrary merely shows how deep and subtle is the vast Welsh conspiracy behind it all. Well, no, actually I don't believe that at all, for the simple reason that any attempt to apportion blame to an individual or to isolate blame onto a particular group or organization is ultimately too simplistic. Governments, banks, political parties, mortgage traders—they are all intertwined in a way that makes such a crisis as we now face a result of a synthesis of mistakes committed by a multitude of miscreants, not the monumental miscalculation of a few.

So why did the markets not stop the problem? After all, according to some conservative pundits, the markets are like the force of gravity—neutral, impersonal, scientific, perpetually moving toward an economic equilibrium that promotes freedom, prosperity, and all-round good health—social, cultural, and above all financial. The answer, of course, is that market forces are ultimately functions of human behavior, albeit on a macro-level; and human beings, being as depraved and as blinded as they are, generate market forces that reflect that depravity. Now, the response will no doubt come from some conservatives that the market actually provides a mechanism for mitigating, or even obliterating, this depravity by the fact that competition leads to a canceling out of depravity. For example, those who argue that the free market will solve environmental problems will make the valid observation that it is in no one's best interest to so pollute the planet that we die

72

of toxic fumes or global warming. So Mrs. Ruth-Less Exploiter, CEO of Megadirt Factories Incorporated, will, by virtue of self-interest, curb her use of fossil fuels because she does not want to live in a world where she can hardly breathe; nor will she be able to sell products made in an environmentally destructive way to the wider public.

The argument, even in the brief and simplistic way I have expressed it here, has a certain specious force. But I would argue that the problem with such arguments is that they take no real account of the radical nature of human depravity. They assume we know what is best for us and how to achieve it; and that, possessing that knowledge, we will abide by it. Both assumptions are woefully naive and unmitigatedly Pelagian. As a human being in rebellion against God, I automatically assume that I am the center of the universe, the measure of all things, that I know best what is good for me and for everyone else, and that "it"—whatever bad thing we care to think of—is not going to happen to me. Indeed, at times, I might even take perverse pleasure in running the risk of "it" happening to me in order to prove that it cannot, and that I am special. You only have to look at the sporadic rise in unprotected promiscuous sex among gay men, even those with an acute understanding that AIDS is an ever-present risk, to see that the thrill of the risk, the ecstasy of the moment, trumps notions of self-preservation and radically distorts our understanding of what is and is not in our best self-interest.

A system that assumes equilibrium and stability can be achieved by my self-interest being curbed, restrained, or even neutralized by your self-interest is woefully naive. It fails to understand the narcissism that lies at the heart of fallen human existence; it fails to understand the fact that hedonism is always a more powerful drive than prudence; and, in its silly belief that competing market forces will neutralize evil, falls vulnerable to that folksy-but-true adage: two wrongs do not make a right.

So who is responsible for the current disaster? We all are. We are all complicit in a world that has increasingly taught people that value in life is a function of the market. This is not a return to the Great Man Theory of history; none of us as an individual carries all responsibility; but just as every mass event in history is both the result of macroeconomic and social forces, and the result of countless individuals behaving in particular ways, so this crisis is both a product of our times, and an action in which we have all had a hand. We are all complicit in creating and fostering a culture of material acquisition, and a world that, in order to ensure insane levels of economic growth, instills insane levels of material aspiration in its people. An easy sell to a fallen race that now naturally exalts greed and hedonism as virtues and sees quality of life in terms of how much we can consume in comparison with others. Every time you turn on the television, somebody is trying to tell you in some commercial or other that your life is imperfect, and it is imperfect because you do not possess this food mixer, that car, this holiday, that size or number of houses. The credit boom is part and parcel of the con game that modern consumer society has played on us, the notion that material acquisition is what makes life meaningful. It has provided the fuel, as untrammeled free market theory has provided the rationale, for the mess in which we now find ourselves. And we are not victims of this; we are all at best hapless and willing dupes, at worst active perpetrators, whether borrowers or lenders; we are all part of a system that is designed simultaneously to satiate greed and exacerbate avarice.

How should Christians respond to all this? I want to sow three thoughts in your minds. First, realize that, while free markets might be the best way of organizing economies at the moment, they are simply the best of a bad lot. Anything human beings create is going to be more or less a mess. Fascism, Communism, feudalism, jihadism—all are worse than what we have, and thus, in relation to these options, I am relatively happy to live where and when I do; but what we have in America is no divinely sanctioned paradise, no foretaste or anticipation of the eschaton. There will be no free markets in heaven (indeed, if the imagery of Revelation 18 is anything to go by, free market philosophy is quite at home on the streets of Babylon!). Free market economies are a provisional and contingent form of economic organization, valid, so it seems, at this moment in time. Are they "the end of history" as some have claimed? Well, to invest them with absolute eschatological significance shows more indebtedness to post-Marxist right-wing Hegelianism than to the Bible.

Second, let's abandon the bombastic bunkum of "the morality of the markets," language that is particularly embarrassing when it comes from the lips of professing Christians. Morality is a predicate of people, not impersonal economic systems. Markets have no morality above and beyond that which is exhibited in the lives of those who buy and sell in them; and as these people are fallen, we should not be surprised that the markets ultimately reflect that fallenness, just as any other human-designed-and-staffed system does. And make no mistake: economic libertarianism and social conservatism are uneasy and volatile bedfellows, whatever the

Christian Right might like to tell you. When you can save money by killing babies in the womb and by euthanizing the old and the weak, and when you can make oodles of dosh by selling designer clothes to the "gay community" and by marketing fragrances bearing the name of a beautiful but promiscuous Hollywood actress, then guess what? In a market-driven world, the case against abortion, euthanasia, homosexuality, and a beauty that is only skin deep and allied to a sleazy lifestyle becomes increasingly difficult to make; indeed, the morality of the market would dictate that a day will come—and perhaps has already come—when it will appear immoral even to try.

Third, let's avoid naive versions of the blame game for the current crisis. I know that saying this will win me few friends, but, frankly, to blame the politicians is to overestimate their importance massively; and the banks could not have done what they did without a large, compliant, and greedy population to jump into the whirlpool of easy credit that they created. The subprime mortgage crisis is a function of a society built on greedy and unrealistic material aspirations. It is the society we have all helped to make, even those who didn't lie on their mortgage applications. We are all guilty. Our greed and the banks' easy credit: the dream team for economic self-destruction. It is not a financial bailout that is needed; it is individual repentance by countless thousands of people.

I see Inspirational Technologies has produced a GPS system that allows you to locate a church of your preference, to avoid those embarrassing moments on holiday when you show up at the first church you come to on the Sunday to find that the lady with the scary hair who is handling those snakes is actually the pastor. . . . At $999 plus tax, the Ecclesiax 500 is not cheap but has a variety of functions. Simply type in a series of preferences and it will take you from where you are to a church where you can feel comfortable. Settings include Atmosphere—from "Friendly" right through to "Reformed"; Worship—choose from "Psalms only," "Traditional," "Hymn-Chorus Mix," "Garage," "Hip Hop," and "Speedcore" (Del—you'll have to clarify those last three for me). Ministers can be specifically profiled, all the way from "Very Traditional" through "Sad Character Suffering Mid-Life Crisis" to the tragic extremes of "Middle Aged but Still Has a Goatee, Earring and Pony Tail." Preaching is categorized from "Proclamation" through "Conversation" to "Liturgical Mime with Strobe Lighting." There's even an option on Christian freedom: from "Drinking and Smoking Forbidden" to "Drinking and Smoking Absolutely Compulsory."

Obviously, the system has certain North American biases: when asking about Cultural Sensitivity, the system gives a range of options from "What?" through to the dizzy cross-cultural heights of "Obtained Passport Six Months Ago."

Still, if you want to beat the consumerist mentality that leads so many to move from church to church on a Sunday, this could be one hot little must-have device that allows you to make the right choice first time, every time.

10

From the Versace Vacuum to the Brand of Brothers

December 2008

WHAT DO THE BRAINLESS and temperamental supermodel, Naomi Campbell, and certain leading figures in American evangelical Christianity have in common? No, I am not thinking of the obvious things: first-class air travel, tantrums, five-star hotels, Narcissistic Personality Disorder, and demands for absolute, unquestioning adulation and obedience from all staff members. I am thinking of something much more subtle and significant than those. Let me explain.

I forget the exact date—sometime in the last decade but probably before 2001, when I arrived in the U.S.A.—Ms. Campbell wrote a novel. To be precise, when I say "wrote," I really mean "didn't write" because what actually happened was that somebody else wrote the book for her, with Campbell merely providing her name on the cover as the alleged author. How do I know this? Well, at the news conference to launch the book, Ms. Campbell was there in all her glory, a veritable vacuum dressed in Versace, to answer questions on her novel; but the answers were somewhat vague and faltering. The reason? She had only been briefed on the content of the book immediately prior to the press conference and thus her knowledge of what she had (not) written was limited entirely to the brief summary provided by her ghostwriter. What was so ridiculous was that all the press present knew about this and, indeed, reported it; they made no attempt to cover up the situation at all; and yet the book was still sold.

Whether the book was any good, I know not, although the fact that Naomi Campbell was willing to have it issued in her name would seem to send strong hints regarding its overall literary quality. John Updike and Joyce Carol Oates need not, I suspect, go looking for day jobs in the face of such fierce competition. What was fascinating was not that Campbell did not write it, but that the book clearly represented the trumping of author as—well—author by author as brand. The book was not written by Her Vacuous Versaceness; but it had her imprimatur. Her name as author represented a kind of apotheosis of the jacket commendation or the Oprah Book Club seal, something that (apparently) made the book marketable.

What has all this to do with certain leading Christian figures? Much in every way. Let me explain. Sometime ago a student brought to my attention a web review of a book I had written. Not recognizing the name of the reviewer, I asked the student who it was. Oh, the student replied, that's (let's call him Rev. Brandon Meganame to protect the—ahem—guilty) Rev. Brandon Meganame's ghostwriter. What? I replied, Rev. Meganame has a ghostwriter? Yes, the student answered. In fact, Rev. Meganame has not written a book for at least a decade. Well, fancy that. Rev. Meganame is not so much an author—in fact, not an author at all in the last decade; he is rather a brand, a logo, the evangelical equivalent of the Lacoste alligator. He doesn't write books; he merely does the evangelical equivalent of lip-synching, more akin to Britney Spears than Martin Luther.

Before I switch my flamethrower to "Total Righteous Destruction," it is worth reflecting for a few moments on the nature of authorship. I am not thinking so much here of the various arguments about authorial intent and the "death of the author" but more about other, related matters. In the nineteenth century and before, it was not uncommon for essays and books to appear anonymously, sometimes identifying the author only by initials, sometimes by phrases that seem today rather quaint, such as "Written by a Gentleman of Quality." The idea behind such authorial modesty would appear to be that the content of the work was of more significance than the one who wrote it. Of course, this is not the only reason an author might use, say, a pseudonym. Mary Ann Evans wrote as George Eliot because she thought a male name would mean her work was taken more seriously; less significantly, perhaps, Eric Blair wrote as George Orwell for the simple reason that he hated the name "Eric." More recently, two of my own favorite authors, Ruth Rendell and Ian Rankin, also write under the names of Barbara Vine and Jack Harvey respectively, although why they do so is a mystery to me, especially since the book covers usually make the identification.

The idea of the ghostwriter is, of course, scarcely unique to Ms. Campbell and the Rev. Meganame. This phenomenon is on full display during the Christmas buying season, as shelves of bookstores are often full of the latest pulp biographies of sports stars and assorted ne'er-do-wells. Indeed, when I was growing up, Christmas didn't seem Christmas without some former gangster, such as the delightful "Mad" Frankie Fraser, producing another lurid volume cataloguing his random acts of violence against fellow villains and the occasional innocent member of the public. Now, "Mad" Frankie may have been useful when it came to inflicting needless pain on other members of the human race, but whatever pain was inflicted through his tortuous prose was no doubt the fault of the person who ghost wrote his various crimes against English literature. That being said, even old East End villains usually marketed their literary wares by describing them on the cover as "written with" or "as told to" plus the name of the ghostwriter.

But what of Lady Campbell and Rev. Brandon Meganame? Clearly, the use of the said names on the said books is that of a brand, pure and simple. Even "Mad" Frankie had to have actually roughed up a few people and then told his ghostwriter what he had done; with Campbell, her connection to the book was so loose that she needed to be briefed on its content immediately prior to the press conference. One can only speculate about the relationship of anything Rev. Meganame may have said or done to that which occurs in the books bearing his moniker.

This is a strange phenomenon, and not simply for its obvious fraudulence and absurdity. It is also surely one of the unnoticed ironies of the postmodern world, at the very point when we are being told that the author is dead and that meaning is in the eye of the beholder or the beholding community, that there is a veritable proliferation of intellectual property laws that define and protect the rights of authors; and also we find this strange phenomenon of the ghostwriter who needs the celebrity author's name to guarantee quality, or at least massively enhance sales. Authors may be dead for epistemological purposes, but their rights are well protected, even if they didn't actually write a word of the book that bears their name; indeed, the author's name on the spine seems today to be critical to making sure some books are successes, as witnessed by the difficulty of new authors breaking into the publishing game. So we have this unholy rise of the ghostwriter who is utterly separable from the author.

As to the first, the so-called "death of the author" in a time of intellectual property rights, I have often thought it would be an interesting experiment in the practical limits of postmodern epistemology for me to plagiarize word-for-word one of the trendy evangelical books advocating postmodern communitarianism as the source of meaning and then see whether the author or publisher dared sue. I can see my defense counsel making his speech now; "But, m'lud, the book says that the meaning of texts is entirely socially constructed; thus, that my client's work and that of Rev. Prof. Dave Trendy are word-for-word the same is neither here nor there; they are actually entirely different works, making two entirely different arguments. Indeed, m'lud, I have two discrete reading communities that I intend to call as witnesses whose testimony will prove beyond any reasonable doubt that my client's authorial intention is entirely different to that of Rev. Trendy and that, in fact, neither his authorial intention nor that of my client are at all relevant to the meaning of said text...." My guess is that the author might well be epistemologically dead;

but said epistemological death would not prevent Dave Trendy from claiming the money, reputation, and status that he believes his self-written, self-referential ideological obituary to deserve.

On the second, the rise of author as brand name, I am concerned that this is clearly making its way into American evangelical culture, even that culture that declares itself to stand in opposition to so many of the exploitative sharp practices of the televangelists and prosperity peddlers. Now, I am the first to admit that some books I buy because of the author's name, particularly in fields that are not my own. I have a general idea of who the reliable evangelical scholars are, who is worth reading on this topic or that in, for example, biblical studies, ethics, and theology; and there is a sense in which, reading far outside my field, I often rely on my knowledge of a particular writer's track record with past books, scholarly reviewers, other people in the field whose opinions I trust, etc. My opinion is shaped not so much by my own expertise in the field but by drawing on what I might call public community resources to establish who is reliable, where weaknesses in arguments might be found, and where original contributions of real merit are made. Thus, there is a sense in which I buy and read the books by these people because I know the brand is reliable; but the brand is critically and inextricably linked to the person and his or her abilities, track record, and reputation for competence.

When the brand gets divorced from these things, when the leader does not just hand a roughly hewn manuscript to an editor who smooths it into a readable and stylish piece of work, then I believe we are moving away from the acceptable canons of literary practice and intellectual ownership into something more sinister, something that lacks integrity and that also capitulates to, or even capitalizes on, one of the most insidious aspects of modern culture: the celebrity brand. I also believe it can involve clear intellectual theft, albeit a kind of ironic theft with permission. The hard work of one person is taken by another and passed off as his own. The writer does not receive the credit he deserves, while the brand name receives unmerited acclaim, and the customer is conned into buying something that is not what it seems to be. It is rather like buying a Pink Floyd album, only to find that the music and the singing have been done by a cover group; all the original band has done is lip-synch. We would regard that as unacceptable in secular pop music, as witness the cases of the awful Milli Vanilli and the unthinkably bad Boney-M. Why should evangelical books be held to a lower standard? Indeed, why should they not be held to a much higher level? Or is this just one more area where Christians are actually in the vanguard of setting new levels of ethical and cultural mediocrity?

Of course, this ties in with one of my pet peeves: that the evangelical subculture simply replicates (usually in a more mediocre way) the practices, values, and behavioral patterns of the advanced consumerist societies in which we live. This is a place where style trumps, or even displaces, substance, and where aesthetic concerns are the ultimate determinants of coherence, plausibility, and value. So much of the tragic impotence of the church today is embodied in the fact that, in her fight against worldliness, she has attacked the obvious enemies such as sexual immorality and public blasphemy, but has done so through cultural idioms that are as worldly as anything out there. The cult of celebrity, with its apotheosis in the arrival of the ghostwriter and the evangelical leader brand name, is not simply an embar-rassment to the evangelical world; it also speaks of a movement that has sold out to the cult of personality.

Tragically, the step from the Versace vacuum to the brand of evangelical brotherhood seems to have been but a small one. Indeed, all this malarkey is enough to make me want to write a book about it; but what's the point? Unless I can get a really big name to claim it as their own and put their name on the spine, it's unlikely that anyone in the evangelical constituency will bother to read it.

11

WELCOME TO WHEREVER
YOU ARE

November 2009

ANYONE WHO HAS ever emigrated as an adult to a foreign country will tell you that, while the physical process of moving can be dispatched in a relatively short period of time, the emotional and cultural transition takes much longer and probably never quite comes to an end. For me, the distance from family was difficult at times, but at least it was something that I knew would be part and parcel of the deal. With cheap phone calls and reasonable transatlantic flights, I probably spend more time in terms of hours at home with my mother now than I have done since graduating from university. What I did not expect were the countless other things, many of them trivial, that I miss and that all serve to make me feel that I remain a British round peg jammed into an American square hole.

Take village pubs, for example, and British beer. Despite the rumors, Americans do make world-class beer. Nevertheless, as good as quality American microbrewed beer is, it is different from what I drink back home in the village pub; and there is never a horse brass, an open fire, or a comfy chair (and rarely a dart board) to be seen in the so-called "British" pubs over here. Indeed, there is nothing that warns that one is about to enter a zone ineradicably marked by Uncle Sam than the adjective "British," "English," or "Irish" before the word "Pub" outside an American establishment. Hanging a picture of the Beatles on the wall, or having shamrock wallpaper and a couple of leprechaun bobbleheads on the bar, simply indicates that, whatever else the establishment is, it bears no resemblance to anything one might find in the old country.

Pubs and beer are simply two examples of the countless cultural disconnects that a British emigrant to the U.S. encounters; most of them relate to such trivial matters; some of them indeed are hard to articulate in any meaningful way; but the cumulative effect can be, if not vertiginously disorienting, then certainly, like that pea under the proverbial mattress in the fairy tale, most definitely irritating. And, lest I seem to be criticizing my host country, I am not; I am simply making an observation; and I am reliably informed that similar feelings mark the experience of Americans in Britain and, indeed, emigrants in general.

One other specific, and perhaps more important, link to the homeland for me and my wife was church. When my family moved to the States in 2001, we left behind a church where I had met my wife as a student, where we had run the youth group together, where I had later served on Session as an elder, and where we not only had many friends but were also blissfully happy. Thus, when we arrived in the States, while we were not homesick in the conventional sense, we both missed the church terribly. Indeed, even now my wife will often say to me that she never feels more like a foreigner in America than during the worship service on Sunday morning, and I feel much the same. Neither of us can articulate why this is so: the worship is in English; and, while the Aberdeen church only sang unaccompanied psalms in contrast with the music and hymns of the Orthodox Presbyterian Church where we now worship, we both agree it is not that; it is just different somehow in an indefinable but very real manner.

The significance of this for me was that, for the first few years in America, I retained my membership in the Free Church and even came under care of a Scottish presbytery with a view to being ordained as a Free Kirk minister. At the time, I justified it by wanting to be a voice for the Free Kirk at Westminster; in retrospect, I realize I was really trying to maintain an emotional tie with my past. Emigration is hard; and it took time for me to come to terms with severing my various connections to home.

In fact, it was not until some years after moving to the U.S. that a minister in the Free Church who happened to be visiting pointed out to me that, as a Christian, I was commanded to love the Body of Christ, and that (a) this was a command, not some sentimental emotional response and (b) the part of the Body of Christ where I now found myself was a congregation of the Orthodox Presbyterian Church. The obvious conclusion, he pointed out, was that I should disregard my nostalgic attachments to the Free Church and commit to the local body. In light of his comments, I slowly came to realize that he was right, and that I needed to make the move.

Thus it is that my wife and I are now members of the OPC. It is where the Lord has placed us, and it is where we are to serve.

There may be bigger churches, there may be better churches, but here is where we find ourselves; here is where the Lord has put us; here is where we are to serve and to love our fellow believers in Christ. I may have a few initials after my name; I may be a seminary professor; I may have published books; but these things make me no better than any other member of the body, and certainly do not exempt me from a proper accounting of my work in the local church where the Lord has put me, whether it is taking out the trash or helping to dismantle the tent after Vacation Bible School. Here is where we are; these are the people among whom we must live and whom we must serve. Indeed, if I happen to preach and some five-year-old child comes up to me afterward and asks me "Who made God?" I must not patronize her, or ignore her, or fob her off with some trite but inadequate pietism; I must answer her question with the seriousness that it deserves. Like all believers, I am called to serve others, and primarily to serve where God has placed me.

Remembering these simple facts about the Christian life can help orient us to priorities. For example, I have been asked by several people over recent years whether Christians should respond if they are criticized or defamed on the web. The answer is simple: for myself, I do not believe that it is appropriate that I spend my time defending my name. My name is nothing—who really cares about it? And I am not called to waste precious hours and energy in fighting off every person with a laptop who wants to have a pop at me. As a Christian, I am not meant to engage in self-justification any more than self-promotion; I am called rather to defend the name of Christ; and, to be honest, I have yet to see a criticism of me, true or untrue, to which I could justifiably respond on the grounds that it was Christ's honor, and not simply my ego, that was being damaged. I am called to spend my time in being a husband, a father, a minister in my denomination, a member of my church, a good friend to those around me, and a conscientious employee. These things, these people, these locations and contexts, are to shape my priorities and my allocation of time. Hitting back in anger at those who, justly or unjustly, do not like me and for some reason think the world needs to know what they think of me is no part of my God-given vocation. God will look after my reputation if needs be; He has given me other work to do.

This realization that the Lord has called me—and I am guessing, most of us—to serve first and foremost wherever we actually are—our families, our congregations, our denominations, and our workplaces—is surely a sobering one. It lacks so much ambition, and shows such a limited vision, after all. Yet in this regard, I think the church is best served by those with such limited ambitions and myopia. I am not much of a web-wanderer but on the odd occasion I do a bit of websurfing, I am struck by how many Christians, pastors, professors, and laity have blogs, Facebook pages, and Twitters going. How many millions of Christian hours are wasted writing this stuff, engaging in mindless blog threads, and telling the world about personal trivia? And what does it tell us about the expansive visions and ambitions out there? Apparently the world is now everyone's birthright.

Now, I find myself very uncomfortable with this. I do believe that some professors, pastors, and laypeople are called to have regular ministries outside their immediate geographical locations; but I also believe that there are precious few thus called. Certainly, mere possession of high-speed Internet is not a divinely given sign of such a worldwide calling. When I see Christians blogging so much, I wonder how many sermons are being prepared on the fly because of lack of time, how many parishioners go unvisited, how many prayers remain unprayed, how many words of love and affection to spouses and children are never said, how many books—let alone the Bible—are left unread, and how many fellowships atrophy through lack of any real, meaningful social and spiritual intercourse. Indeed, to summarize: how many online "communities" (sic) prosper to the detriment of the real, physical communities into which the Lord has placed each and every one of us? How many complain of insufficient time to do the boring routines of the Christian life—worship services, Sunday school, visiting the sick and the aged, fellowship, Bible reading, prayer—and yet always somehow manage to fit in a quick twitter or blog or podcast or change to their Facebook status?

I am increasingly convicted of my own failures in this regard. The Internet has never been my particular temptation; to me the web has been—and, indeed, remains—basically a quick means to shop. Beyond that, it is simply an ironic-to-absurd medium in the way in which it allows everybody, regardless of sanity, IQ, or qualifications, to have their fifteen seconds of fame. Frankly, 95 percent of it is utterly ridiculous as far as I can judge, the denizens of webworld being akin to the institution described in Edgar Allan Poe's tale, *The System of Doctor Tarr and Professor Fether.* Yet, if the web has not consumed my time, then traveling has perhaps been my particular weakness, combined with a general inability to say "no" to any request to help with preaching or lecturing. The net result is that I have probably ministered all over the place, but not so much in the church congregation where the Lord has actually placed me, that part of the Body of Christ that I am particularly obliged to love and encourage and to which I am accountable. Of course, being there of all places will never make me a superstar or a guru or earn me a fortune or get me a cool conference gig or land me on the cover of *Christianity Today*; but it is nonetheless the place where I am meant to be.

The command to love the Body of Christ is indeed a command, not a sentiment. It comes with specific demands on time and on place. I pray that I will learn more and more about what these demands truly mean. And I pray too that more and more Christians will come to realize that real life is lived in the real world in the real church where they really attend on a Sunday. Time to get out of the system of Doctor Tarr and Professor Fether and join the real world.

Welcome to wherever you are.

12

WHY ARE THERE NEVER ENOUGH PARKING SPACES AT THE PROSTATE CLINIC?

January 2009

ONE OF THE MODERN shibboleths of the evangelical church, particularly the evangelical church in the West, is that of culture. One must be interested in culture, or one is simply irrelevant. Books and organizations abound on Christian approaches to various aspects of modern culture; there are magazines and e-zines dedicated to the topic; and numerous conferences are held—some local, some national, some international—that address cultural issues in terms of the categories and so-called world and life view of Christianity. Now, I don't want to throw the baby out with the bathwater: sure, we need to understand the language and idioms of our culture to the extent that we need to communicate the gospel in such a context in a meaningful, comprehensible way; but I do believe that fascination with culture is now way out of hand in Christian circles and has come to eclipse more important, more central things. Indeed, even as I say that it is important to understand context to communicate the gospel effectively, I am conscious that this seemingly obvious statement needs to be tempered by the fact that some of the greatest preaching ever known was designed precisely not to communicate to the contemporary culture. Just check Isaiah's commission in Isaiah 6, and the use of that text in Jesus' ministry to see how not communicating in comprehensible categories as determined by the immediate culture is a critical sign of judgment on an idolatrous people.

Space prevents me from engaging in a thoroughgoing engagement with the current obsession of Christians with culture; but I would like, as it were, to sketch out the framework of a minority report on the matter by highlighting a series of concerns.

First, I am struck, by and large, with the coincidence of the concerns of the cultural Christian types and those of the middle-class chatterati: plenty of talk about Christian approaches to art, music, literature, sex, even international politics. They are all very interesting subjects, I'm sure, and the topics of many a chardonnay-fueled discussion after a hearty dinner party. But what about subjects that aren't quite so interesting? Take street sweepers, for example; or hotel lavatory attendants; or workers on an umbrella manufacturing line. Why no conference on the Christian philosophy underlying these vital callings and trades? After all, imagine how gruesome a Christian conference on international poverty would be if it were held in the pouring rain in the Ritz-Carlton hotel in some big city, but there were no road sweepers, lavatory attendants, and umbrella makers. Wet, dirty, and unhygienic, I would guess.

Second, I am also struck by how Christian talk of cultural engagement has coincided with a watering-down of Christian standards of behavior and, ironically, thought. I have lost count of how many times I have been told in recent years that Christians should be able to watch any movie, providing they do so with a critical, Christian eye. There are several obvious problems with that kind of statement. For a start, such a categorical, sweeping statement has little, if any, scriptural or exegetical foundation, and indeed seems not to take any account of texts such as Matthew 5:27–30; Ephesians 5:1–3; Philippians 4:8, etc. Second, even those making the case rarely mean exactly what they say: ask them whether Christians can therefore watch child pornography, and none that I have spoken to have been prepared to go that far, except in the necessary cases of those professionally involved in the detection and prosecution of pedophile crime. No, Christians shouldn't watch child porn, they'll say; but the problem, of course, is that definitions of what is and is not pornography, even child pornography, are changing all the time and are driven, by and large, by the wider culture that increasingly mainstreams such material. Witness a recent Kate Winslet movie involving a sex scene between her character and a fifteen-year-old boy. Specious distinctions involving the actual age of the actor notwithstanding, it is arguably child pornography. Frankly, there are films rated PG-13 today that my grandparents would have considered as porn. Is the standard of what is and is not obscene set by biblical truth or by cultural accommodation? Talk of "Christians can watch anything as long as they do it critically" is as daft, unbiblical, soft-headed, ill-thought-out, and confused as anything one is likely to come across. In fact, I have a suspicion that for some it might simply function as a rationalization for watching whatever they like and not having to feel guilty about it, the Christian voyeur's equivalent of the "I only do screen nudity and sex when the script demands it" excuse of so many "serious" actresses whose bank balances have been boosted by the occasional flash of on-screen flesh.

But the change in Christian thinking does not just relate to issues like pornography. It also relates to the very questions that are deemed relevant or useful. I always thought it was the Bible that was meant to interrogate the culture; but the order seems to be reversing somewhat in recent times. For example, a few years ago Mel Gibson's film, *The Passion of the Christ*, was all the rage in evangelical circles. One day, I was sitting in my office and a student came by to let me know he was taking the youth group at his church to see it and to ask whether I had already done so. I said I had not, and we then entered a discussion about whether it was right to depict Christ visually on the big screen. At the end of the discussion, he said that he felt sorry for me because my qualms about the visual depiction of Christ were making me irrelevant to ministry in the modern church. Now I may well be irrelevant, although I think time has proved Gibson's *Passion* to be pretty irrelevant as well. What shocked me in this encounter, however, was not that we had different views on the matter, but that the student could not even see that there was any question to be asked. For him, the question of the meaning, relevance, and application of the second commandment was not even a question. He just thought it was obvious that anything that generated interest in Jesus was a good thing; thus, my concerns about the visual depiction of Christ revealed me as an irrelevant old hack, a superannuated Puritan who simply didn't get it. To me, this was a most dramatic symbol of how culture had come to set the theological agenda even within a conservative, confessional, reformed tradition, and to define the plausibility structures not simply of the answers but even of the questions. My question arose out of my concern to see what the Bible said to our cultural situation, and that refracted through centuries of discussion of this point; but this student did not even have the categories to see that there was any question to be asked.

Third, I am convinced that much culture talk is driven by the need to hyperspiritualize everything. Of course, I believe everything should be done to the glory of God; but that doesn't mean I believe we need a Christian theory of movies any more than we need a Christian theory of cake baking, homebrewing, or street sweeping. When I arrive home at night, I sometimes just want to sit down, have a drink, and relax while listening to a piece of music or watching a movie or reading a good book. Pascal was right when he saw that such entertainment was perfectly legitimate in and of itself, when it helped one recover from the drudge and dreariness of the daily grind; when such things become an obsession, an idol, then, of course, they become a problem; but there was no need to specifically Christianize them at a theoretical or epistemological level. Strange to tell, the contemporary evangelical urge to Christianize everything is in itself arguably a form of the very pietism it seeks to reject, where only specifically and consciously Christian things have any legitimate place. Pietism has simply been broadened, not abolished.

Fourth, I am increasingly convinced that talking about culture, for all of its loud claims to relevance, significance, and importance, can actually be a first-class way of doing precisely the opposite, of not really talking about things that matter at all. After all, at root, talk about culture is talk about accidents. No, I don't mean that culture talk is always talk about unfortunate disasters: no cultural critic with whom I am acquainted spends the whole time discussing Britney Spears, *The O'Reilly Factor*, and Wales. What I mean is that talk about culture is talk about particulars rather than universals, local differences rather than transcendent unifiers, and accidental properties rather than natural essences. This kind of disposition lies at the heart of postmodern thought: postmoderns hate to talk about nature and essence because that would imply metanarratival totalizing; they have replaced the old discourse of unified nature with the discourse of heterogeneous cultures.

The disempowering and anarchic effect of this shift from nature to culture, from universals to particulars, can be seen dramatically in what has happened on the European political Left. In the 1950s and 1960s, the Left moved from its traditional metanarrative of economic oppression and liberation to concern for identity politics. The categories then ceased to be class-based or related to basic economic structures and hierarchies, and moved to issues of gender, race, and sexuality. In making this shift, the Left lost its universals in a medley of competing particulars. The result is what we have today: a Left that is morally impotent, as revealed first and perhaps most dramatically by responses to the Iranian revolution of 1979. Should the Left support it as the overthrow of a corrupt and brutal American-backed dictatorship, or oppose it as a return to feudalism fueled by religious fanaticism? As the liberation of an ethnic people from Western imperialism, or the establishment of a regime whose brutal subjugation of women beggared belief? The embarrassing spectacle of Michel Foucault approving the events in Tehran in 1979 is a nasty specter that should haunt the mind of any who claim to be his disciples or claim him as a man of the true Left, the Left that speaks up for the poor, the oppressed, and the weak. The same confusion has played out again and again in responses to the suppression of Solidarity in Poland, to Tiananmen Square, to 9/11, to war on the Taliban, to the toppling of Saddam Hussein.

As the Left lost itself in a morass of micronarratives and identity politics, it lost its ability to speak with any authority about things that matter; indeed, it lost its ability even to see the things that matter. The universities that should have been centers of serious discussion of things that really matter descended into trivia, losing sight of the basics of politics in an arcane mass of rebarbative theoretical gobbledygook, gnostic vocabulary, and utter trivia. PhDs reflecting on the oppression of the poor came to be replaced with dissertations on cybersex, foot fetishists, and, no doubt at some point, the semiotic importance of Tom Jones impersonators. The margins became central; the center, unable to hold, was thrust to the margins; and the Left became an irrelevance to changing the things that really matter.

As this postmodern ethos has bled into Christian theology, a similar theological disempowerment has become evident. What began as a healthy concern to contextualize theology led in many cases to theologies where the particulars of context (whether geographical, social, political, ethnic, gender, sexual orientation, etc., etc.) effectively trumped the universal horizon of Scripture. The perfect storm of anarchic postmodern philosophies, identity politics, hyperspecialization and fragmentation of the theological discipline, fear of cultural irrelevance, and the eclectic mind-set of the consumer have combined to create a situation where the particular rules, messiness is in, and the church is little more than a cacophony of competing voices (or, to use the trendy and pretentious terminology, "dissonant vocalities"). On every corner, huckster theologians who have made their careers out of creating this mess are selling you the problem as if it is the solution, and theology now abounds with Orwellian newspeak: chaos is order; contradiction is consistency; valueless trivia is vital truth. And the Christian culture vultures are at the cutting edge of this, with their focus on the particular and the peripheral rather than the universal and the central. Kids' stuff—teenflicks and sex and the Internet—holds center stage in so much Christian cultural conversation, perhaps a sign of the West's obsession with all things adolescent, perhaps a sign of the permanent adolescence of many of the interlocutors. And let's face it, no one ever loses in today's evangelical market by backing the peripheral rather than the central, or by overestimating the triviality of the tastes of the Western Christian consumer. Is a Christian bookstore going to make money selling a book on the Incarnation or on prayer, or one on Christian approaches to body image, or *The Simpsons*, or how to improve your sex life?

You can test this appetite for trivia easily. Today, more people in church are less familiar with the basics of the Bible and Christian theology than ever before; so you should ask your pastor to arrange some parallel seminars on a Saturday with one on, say, the elements of the Apostles' Creed, and one on a Christian approach to movies or sex. I guarantee you that the second will be far better attended than the first. Peripheral trivia trumps central truth every time, even within the ranks of the orthodox consumers in our churches.

So much for the rant. Where do I go from here? Well, in a day when identity politics is in, I have decided to launch my own webzine, aimed specifically at that most neglected sector of today's culture: miserable middle-aged gits, of whom I am a foremost representative. To capture the essence of the project, I am going to call it "Oi You, Get Off My Lawn!" as long as the relevant web address (www.oiyougetoffmylawn.com) is not taken. I'll have a regular monthly column on today's music scene, called "Call That Music?? They Don't Write Them Like They Used To." I'll have a section devoted to political commentary, "It Would Never Have Happened in My Day." There'll probably be a sidebar on youth culture, titled, "I Ask You, Kids Today! They Don't Know They're Born." And, finally, there'll be a regular editorial, addressing such urgent issues of the day as "Dooyeweerd or Don't You Weird? The Case Against Soul Patches," and "Why Are There Never Enough Parking Spaces at the Prostate Clinic? Toward a Christian Response." Now, if you don't think these columns and questions are relevant, then you must be either (a) a woman or (b) a man under the age of 40. If the latter, give it a few years and the profound relevance of these issues will become painfully clear. In the meantime, don't oppress me by engaging in the imperialist, sexist, modernist, foundationalist, miserablemiddleagedgitophobic etc., etc. marginalizing of "the Other"—i.e., me and my pals—in order to make your own little world the norm. Miserable middle-aged gits we may be, but we have a right to our culture and our own local narrative too! We have been silenced by the oppressors for too long.

Alternatively, I could try to move out of my own little world, start thinking less in cultural and more in biblical terms. I could become less obsessed with particularities and more concerned with universals. I could engage less with the accidents of culture and more with the substance of nature. I might even spend less time training people who don't know the Apostles' Creed to watch movies that would have made grandma blush and more time teaching them the basic elements of Scripture and doctrine. Horribly modernist, I know; in fact, boringly passé. But it might, just might, prove more relevant in the long run than being able to understand the sacramental significance of Sharon Stone or playing "Spot the Redeemer Figure" in the latest Jim Carrey movie.

The August edition of *Reformed Man Today* leads with a shocking story:

The Christian world has today been thrown into turmoil by the discovery of what is probably the earliest MS of J. Gresham Machen's seminal tome, *Christianity and Liberalism*. What is so shocking is that it is now apparent that the original title was *Christianity and Evangelicalism*! Dr. Diogenes Altleben, of the Dept. of Lederhosen at the University of Wienerschnitzel, declared that this was "proof positive zat Vestminster, from its veeeerrrry inception, defined itself not against ze liberals but against ze evangelicals!"

Lawyers for Fredo "the Bull" Schleiermacher, feared in the evangelical underworld as "the Godfather of Liberalism," and who is currently serving a four-hundred-year sentence for the contract killing of Christian Orthodoxy on behalf of a cultural despiser who was never identified at his trial, declared that they now plan to lodge an appeal against his conviction and press for his immediate release.

Interviewed in his prison cell, Fredo Schleiermacher said yesterday, "I knew it was them conservative evangelicals wot dunnit all along. I mean, I woz fitted by the old bill and the Odge Gang, with their enlightenment foundationalism and their common sense, wozn't I? My only crime was to reduce all Christian doctrinal claims to statements of the religious psychology of the individual and to take the odd bung from religion's cultured despisers. Nobody got 'urt and everyone woz 'appy. Believe me, when I get out, somebody's gonna get sued."

Ludwig Feuerbach was unavailable for comment.

13

TRAPPED IN NEVERLAND

November 2008

GROWING UP, I adored my grandfather. He was probably the funniest man I ever knew, with a razor-sharp wit, absurdism and satire running through his veins, and an imagination that seemed to know no bounds. His letters to me were mini-masterpieces of surreal satire, and he knew how to have fun, how to puncture pomposity, and how to provoke people to think. Yet he was, by today's standards, uneducated. He had left school at thirteen to work in a factory; he was a union man; he lived through the General Strike and the Depression; he knew what it was like to tramp the streets, looking for work but knowing there was no work to be found; and, a psychological victim of the British class system, he never came to see my mum play sport for her school lest he cause her embarrassment. I loved him dearly, and when he died, it was as if my own world came to an end.

I hated the system that had treated my grandfather like dirt and kept him tugging his forelock at those whose only virtue was to have been born to wealthier families; I hated the system that had worked him so hard and broken his health so that he could never really enjoy his retirement; and I hated the system that had made him believe all this was part of his proper place in the world and had even convinced him that it would be less embarrassing for all if he did not come to the touchline to watch his daughter play sport for her school. Indeed, one of the reasons I wanted so desperately to get into Cambridge was to show him, and myself, and the chinless public school (in the British sense) wonders who epitomized the system, that the system could be beaten, that someone from my family could push his way into the very heart of the establishment by sheer hard work and natural talent, rather than by money, "breeding," and possession of no chin and an old school tie. The day I was accepted, he told my mum that he could not believe that the family had risen from being nothing to being represented at Cambridge. But in my eyes we hadn't risen at all, we had simply made a necessary point: we could do it too; we could get to where "they" were. My grandfather was not nothing; he was—and still is—one of the greatest men I have ever known. What could that great mind have done, if only it had been given the privilege and leisure of study?

Now, there's quite a contrast between the world in which my grandfather grew up and the world of today. By age fifteen, he had done two years of hard work; had he not done so, the result would have been simple—he would have starved. By age twenty, he knew what responsibility was; by age thirty he had spent over half his life in the workplace. Indeed, he did not become an adult when he married and had children; he had already been an adult since before he had really needed to shave.

Today is so different. If the poverty and hard work of my grandfather's era left men middle-aged at thirty, the ease and trivia of today's society seem to leave us trapped in a permanent Neverland where we all, like so many Peter (and Patty) Pans, live lives of eternal youth. Whereas my grandfather spent his day hard at work, trying—sometimes desperately—to make enough money to put bread on the table and shoes on his children's feet, today many have time to play X-Box and video games, or warble on and on incessantly in that narcissistic echo chamber that is the blogosphere. The world of my grandfather was evil because it made him grow up too fast; the world of today is evil because it prevents many from ever growing up at all.

In some ways, today's world is the very antithesis of earlier ages. I always found sixteenth- and seventeenth-century paintings of children to be somewhat creepy: adult heads on tiny, immature bodies, as if the artists had no real concept of youth and childhood that allowed them to depict faces as such. Strange, isn't it, that the airbrushing techniques so often used in today's glossy magazines seem designed to have precisely the opposite effect: to place young heads on bodies that we know are much older. The concept of old age is perhaps slowly but surely being airbrushed out of representations in the popular media.

Numerous incidents over recent years have brought the sad effect of all this home to me. As a professor at university and seminary, I have had too many run-ins with students who act like five-year-olds and, when held to account, express all the pouting resentment that one comes to expect from a generation that demands respect but refuses to put in the time and effort to earn it. You see them on the blogs, screaming their abuse and demanding to be heard, carrying on their tirades long after the threshold of Godwin's Law and any semblance of decency or credibility has been passed for the umpteenth time. They have achieved nothing—but they demand that you respect them!

The inept Islamic suicide bombers in Britain are just the most extreme, pestiferous example of this immaturity: incompetent, spotty juveniles who make portentous suicide videos and then fail to blow anything up because they forgot their car keys, or bought the wrong ingredients for bomb making from the local store, or were amazed that putting in an order for two hundred bottles of peroxide aroused suspicion at the local hair salon, whose owner contacted the police: "I see, madame, and can I assume that Mr. Mohammed is not actually a natural blond . . . ?" These thugs demand respect in the most extreme ways; but their behavior inspires less horror than it does simple derision and mockery.

But it gets more disturbing than simply finding people in their twenties and thirties acting like spoiled children. Parents are becoming increasingly involved as well. With two sons in travel football (that's soccer to any American readers), I have stood on too many touchlines where parents act like frustrated two-year-olds as the game does not develop as they would like; and, again, as a professor, I have had unpleasant experiences with parents too. Being told by a parent that a child is "young and immature" works for my wife—she teaches at a church nursery, dealing with three-year-olds—but it wears a bit thin when the problem child is eighteen, nineteen, twenty . . . thirty. . . . And that this kind of stuff seems more common in the church than in the secular world is disturbing. It does not inspire much confidence about the future and, if anything, provides anecdotal confirmation to those who see religion in general, and Christianity in particular, as a refuge for the emotionally retarded.

So what are we to do? I am tempted to say: return to the world of my grandfather! But that would be foolish. I hated that world for what it did to him. Yes, he grew up fast and took responsibility for himself and his family, but at what cost? Indeed, I hate that world as much as I despise the glib talk of "the dignity of manual labor" that drips from the lips of the chardonnay-sipping chatterati for whom manual labor is not scrubbing floors to make ends meet, as it was for my grandmother, but pruning the roses and putting out the recycle bin once a week—no doubt full of empty bottles of Bolly and Krug.

The answer, then, is not a naive, nostalgic hankering for a return to an era of poverty and cruel hardship. Rather, it is surely obvious: we need to put aside childish things and start acting like adults. Pascal put his finger on the problem of human life when he saw how entertainment had come to occupy a place, not as the necessary and momentary relief from a life of work, but as an end in itself. When entertainment becomes more than a pleasant and occasional distraction, when time and income become devoted to entertainment and to pleasure, when sports teams become more important to us than people—even the people to whom we are close—then something has gone badly wrong. The frothy entertainment culture in which we live is a narcotic: not only is it addictive, so that we always want more; it also eats away at us, skewing our priorities, rotting our values as surely as too much sugar rots our teeth. My grandfather was lucky in this one thing: he did not have time to be immature because he did not have the surplus income that would have granted him the luxury. That is not to exalt the virtue of poverty—poverty is an evil—but it is to underscore the dangers that come with wealth in abundance.

Second, we need to stop idolizing our children. At twenty-seven, I had a wife, a child, a PhD, and a monograph from Oxford University Press. I looked for all the world like an adult. Then I got myself into a bit of financial difficulty, to the tune of about two hundred pounds, a small sum but not when you are at the bottom of the British academic pay scale and a one-income family to boot. I phoned my father for help. He read me the riot act about financial irresponsibility, helped me get out of the immediate fix, and told me that he never, ever wanted me to call and tell him I was in such a fix again. He loved me but he did not idolize me; he knew it was time for me to stand on my own two feet. I loved my dad, but he scared the daylights out of me with that talk. Yet, looking back, that was one of the moments that was the making of me: look, son, you're a big boy now; look after yourself and don't come crying to me every time you screw up. A sobering, critical moment in the relationship between father and son; but, in my dealings with others, it finds increasingly few parallels. Touch the child—even the one with the beard, the wisdom teeth, and the warm fuzzy memories of the time when New Kids on the Block were all the rage in high school—and you touch the sacred idol; you can expect the parents to come a-calling.

You are, of course, what you worship, as Psalm 115 reminds us, and thus, as long as we idolize our children and the culture of youth, we can expect to—well, be just like them: pouting, irresponsible, hormonal, unpleasant and, frankly, as creepy as those sixteenth-century portraits of little children with adult faces. Trapped in Neverland with no hope of escape.

14

AN UNMESSIANIC SENSE
OF NONDESTINY

April 2010

FOR MANY MEN of a certain age, the mid-life crisis is
just that: a mid-life crisis, a time for despairing that youth, good
looks, and perhaps hair have gone, never to return. For me, however, the experience has been pretty positive so far: not only
have I been able to hand down my old banger of a car to my
oldest son (thus making myself the greatest dad in the world),
but I've also broken with my lifelong habit of driving pieces of
junk until they disintegrate, and purchased an inexpensive but
decent sports car. Not quite sure how my wife let me get away
with it; but the fact that my previous car leaked when it rained
and the present Mrs. T had told me that enough was enough,
and she was no longer prepared to be "dripped on" as we drove
along in a storm one day, seemed to open up a great opportunity
for sneaking a good car onto the driveway. As she rolled her eyes,

she did say to me that a husband with a decent-looking car is, from her perspective, better than one with a secret girlfriend and/or a not-so-secret toupee. I had to agree: there are indeed much worse forms of the mid-life crisis out there.

One other aspect of my MLC, and one that I have found extraordinarily helpful, is the death of ambition that, in my experience, it seems to have brought in its wake. The realization that one cannot be the best at everything, or even those things at which one used to be the best, is presumably a factor in quite a few MLCs; and for me this was a welcome liberation. I woke up one day a few years ago at the age of forty, and realized that, if I were hit by a bus that night, whatever academic contribution I was ever going to make had already been made; I had done it; I need not worry about it anymore. I could, of course, continue grinding the stuff out, like some intellectual sausage machine; but it would be more of the same, variations on a theme I had already played. No, an early Trueman death would not deprive the world of some great insight it might otherwise miss. I knew I would continue to write and even to do research, but I would do these for the pleasure I found in them, not because I believed it was my God-given task to enrich the waiting world with my pearls of wisdom.

This inner peace reminded me a little of the mental health statistics when I was at university. These indicated that good mental health was generally strongest among us intellectual middle-of-the-packers who were happy with whatever results we achieved: if we scored high, that was a bonus; if we crashed to earth, that was a bit of a blow but nothing too serious; we sailed on in our own, carefree way, not allowing work to interfere too much with trips to the pub, the odd game of darts or pool, and the general enjoyment of life. By contrast, breakdowns and suicides were most common among the intellectually brilliant high-fliers, those for whom nothing less than perfection was acceptable.

So it is with the MLC brigade. There are those for whom the diminution of their intellect, musculature, looks, and hair is a traumatic and desperate experience; and they find nothing that seems to compensate. You can point to the growth of hair in nostrils and ears as much as you like, but, trust me, these men will take no consolation from the fact that their overall number of active follicles remains relatively stable.

For me, and I hope for others, being on the cusp of middle age has, contrary to the above, proved liberating. The key, I believe, is to match diminishing abilities and opportunities with diminishing ambition; balance the former with the latter, and you achieve a sort of zen consciousness where middle age does not seem so terrible after all.

Of course, the acquisition of such consciousness is really somewhat countercultural: not only does today's world consider aging, and the inevitable physical weakening that comes with it, as sins; it also teaches us that everyone is special, has a unique contribution to make, and must have a prize of some kind. All people need to tell the world about their greatness, their uniqueness. It reminds me of the legendary football manager, Brian Clough, who, when asked whether he was the best manager in the world, famously replied, "No, but I'm somewhere in the top one." He was funny because he was one of a kind; but we are all Cloughs now, with the cultural term for those who lack confidence in their unique brilliance being, so I believe, "loser."

This belief that we are each special is, by and large, complete tosh. Most of us are mediocre, make unique contributions only in the peculiar ways we screw things up, and could easily be replaced as husband, father, or employee by somebody better suited to the task. The mythology nevertheless helps to sell things and allows us to feel good about ourselves; indeed, the older you get, the more things it sells, from gym memberships, to cosmetic surgery, to hairpieces, to botox injections; but it is just mythology—the whole of human history so far strongly suggests that, as you get old, you cease to be as cool, and you inevitably find that life just isn't as sweet as it was when you were eighteen.

As I look round the church, it strikes me that this zen-like condition of a lack of ambition is much to be desired because far too many Christians have senses of destiny that verge on the messianic. The confidence that the Lord has a special plan and purpose just for them shapes the way they act and move. Now, just for the record, I am a good Calvinist, and I certainly believe each individual has a destiny; what concerns me is the way in which our tendency to think of ourselves as special and unique (which we all are in some ways—DNA, etc.) bleeds over into a sense of special destiny whereby the future, or at least the future of myself, comes to be the priority and to trump all else.

Put bluntly, when I read the Bible it seems to me that the church is the meaning of human history; but it is the church as a corporate body, not the distinct individuals who make up her membership. Of course, all of us individuals have our gifts and our roles to play: the Lord calls us each by name and numbers the very hairs of our heads; but, to borrow Paul's analogy of the body, we have no special destiny in ourselves taken as isolated units, any more than bits of our own bodies do in isolation from each other. When I act, I act as a whole person; my hand has no special role of its own; it acts only in the context of being part of my overall body. With the church, the destiny of the whole is greater than the sum of the destinies of individual Christians.

This is an important insight that should profoundly shape our thinking and, indeed, our praying. My special destiny as a believer is to be part of the church; and it is the church that is the big player in God's wider plan, not me. That puts me, my uniqueness, my importance, my role, in definite perspective. The problem today is that too many have the idea that God's primary plan is for them, and the church is secondary, the instrument to the realization of their individual significance. They may not even realize they think that way but, like those involuntary "tells" at a poker game, so certain unconscious spiritual behaviors give the game away.

Take, for example, prayer. Compare the prayers that many of us have no doubt prayed, of the "O Lord, please use me for doing X" variety, with the priorities of the Lord's Prayer, where the petition is much more modest—"lead me not into temptation, deliver me from evil, for the kingdom is yours, etc." One could paraphrase that prayer perhaps as follows: "Lord, keep me out of trouble and don't let me get in the way of the growth of your kingdom." No basis there for the typical "Lord, use me greatly to do this, that, or the other thing I quite fancy doing"—usually prayed, of course, before or after the pious throat-clearing phrase, "if it be your will . . . ." The Lord's Prayer, by contrast with many we cook up for ourselves, is a great example of words designed for the lips of believers who really understand the gospel, of those with, to coin a phrase, an unmessianic sense of nondestiny.

Then, think about church commitment. Many churches require members to take vows when they join, one of which usually requires submission to the authority of elders and a commitment to the local body. This church vow is surely one that is as casually taken as it is regularly broken. How many Christians move membership from one church to another as soon as their pet issue or problem is not addressed, or because they see a better option elsewhere? And I have not even mentioned the countless Christians who attend churches but never formally join. Once you shift membership from one church for no reason other than that it doesn't scratch your itch, or stroke you as you would like, it becomes a whole lot easier to do it again—and again, and again. But if you have an unmessianic sense of nondestiny, this is unlikely to be a problem: you won't consider yourself important enough to justify breaking a solemn, public vow.

The West worships the individual; from the cradle to the grave it tells us all how special and unique each of us is, how vital we are to everything, how there is a prize out there just for us. Well, the world turned for thousands of years before any of us showed up; it will continue turning long after we've gone, short of the parousia; and even if you, me, or the Christian next door are hit tonight by an asteroid, kidnaped by aliens, or sucked down the bathroom plughole, very little will actually change; even our loved ones will somehow find a way to carry on without us. We really are not that important. So let's drop the pious prayers, which translate roughly as "Lord, how can a special guy/gal like myself help you out some?" and pray rather that the Lord will grow his kingdom despite our continual screwups, that he will keep us from knocking over the furniture, and that, when all is said and done, somehow, by God's grace, we will finish well despite our best efforts to the contrary.

Mid-life crises are dreaded by many men, but my advice is: gents, seize with both hands the opportunity to truly grasp that, whatever you thought at age eighteen, you are not actually the messiah and you have no special destiny that sets you apart from everybody else. The former is Christ alone; the latter is primarily reserved for his church. We all need to cultivate that certain unmessianic sense of nondestiny that will make us better citizens of the kingdom.

15

OLD OPIUM MEETS THE NEW

June 2008

WELL, WHO WOULD HAVE THOUGHT that it would be Pope Benedict XVI who provided one of the strangest "only in America, folks" moments of recent years. Yet it is undoubtedly true that he has done so. Benedict is, of course, a pope whose medieval predilections, whether theological, liturgical, or merely sartorial, are well known. Indeed, some of the more eye-catching outfits he has worn since assuming his current role look like things that any Borgia pope would have been happy to have donned for an official engagement. And yet, when preparing to address a crowd of 20,000 young people in the U.S. in April, this most medieval of church monarchs was preceded on stage by Ms. Kelly Clarkson, chanteuse. For those fortunate enough to be completely ignorant of the identity of Ms. Clarkson, she was launched on her path to fame by the TV reality series, *American Idol,* a competition in which viewers are allowed to phone in and select the winner of a national talent competition for aspiring singers.

121

Support bands are, of course, an established tradition in the world of popular entertainment. Some eighteen months ago, I took my boys to see The Who (or what is left of them) in Philadelphia. To my great delight, The Pretenders (fronted by the ever-dynamic Chrissie H) were the support band. Twenty odd years ago, I saw U2 at Wembley; their support was provided by Lou Reed and The Pogues. Quite breathtaking, I remember; and thankfully before Bono began to believe his own messianic publicity. So why, I ask myself, could the pope not do better than a former *American Idol* winner when looking for a warm-up act/support band for the American leg of his world tour?

Of course, it made perfect sense. For here I saw the old opium of the people, religion, appropriating the new opium of the people, bland commercialized pop culture. It was Karl Marx, of course, who famously dismissed religion in such terms. By promising the poor, the needy, the suffering, and the oppressed that their reward would be in heaven, religion functioned as one almighty con game perpetrated by the ruling class on those whom they wished to keep in a state of subservience. Don't try to better your lot by rebellion, so the story went, for in doing so you'll forfeit the reward that your suffering and subservience are earning for you in heaven. Thus, the class conflict was defused by the oppressed believing a lie. Marx went so far in *Das Kapital* to name and shame Thomas Chalmers for the charitable works he did in Glasgow, as these were simply one more way of numbing the pain of the oppressed and keeping them from wanting to change their lot in life.

I have over the years found Marx helpful in this matter, not because I agree with his analysis but because he has helped me to see that culture is never value-neutral but is always part of a wider

agenda. Of course, in terms of detail his analysis is tendentious—
I think it is now clear that class struggle and the movement of
capital is not the dynamic of history—and religion of the old kind
is remarkably passé. Yet the critical spirit he represents is useful.
For example, a modern-day Marx, faced with our increasingly
secular world where promises of the afterlife are not as tempting as those of a more material kind, would argue that there are
numerous other "opiums" that distract people from the reality
of their condition, material and spiritual. Take, for example, the
proliferation of lotteries and gambling. These play in part to the
idea that anyone can get rich, that our financial hardships can
be relieved by the purchase of a cheap, winning ticket. In fact, if
you buy a lottery ticket, your chances of winning are only slightly
greater than mine; and mine are zero, because I never purchase
them. Even in a casino, the chances are small. Meyer Lansky, the
Jewish gangster and casino owner (and, I believe, original for
Hyman Roth in *The Godfather II*), warned his own friends never
to gamble as the odds were always with the banker; black jack, he
said, was the best bet, with a 16 percent chance of winning! Yet
people still gamble; people still believe the dream; people still
think happiness can be achieved by a roll of the dice. And if you
can gamble a day's wages in the casino with the chance of millions,
you won't be using that time and money to change the world.

Another opium contender might be the obsession of society
at large with sport. Now I love sport. I really love sport. I run, I
bike, I go to the gym far more than is decent for a middle-aged
balding guy who should simply accept the aging process and sit
at home on a cold morning in January. And I love to watch rugby
on the TV. Yet for me, physical exercise serves to keep me feeling

physically and mentally sharp in the midst of a stressful job; the spectating provides a few moments of occasional relaxation at the weekend. They are instrumental to helping me do the more important things of life in a better way. For many, though, sport has become an integral part of their identity, and, more often than not, it is watching sport, not actual participation, that does this. The success or failure of a team becomes the vicarious success or failure of the supporter. In other words, sport becomes a means of finding authenticity and value. Other areas of life can be neglected, malfunction, or simply go to the dogs; but as long as "the team" is doing well, all is OK with the world. Indeed, in good "opium" fashion, we can be enduring all kinds of garbage being dropped on us; but the "team" gives us hope—albeit specious and illusory—of fulfillment and happiness.

Yet there is one modern opium of the masses that stands above all the others—indeed, which subsumes and consumes these others, in its comprehensive reach, its easy accessibility, its banal content, and its ruthless emasculation of anything radical or prophetic. It is television. Here, in an endless diet of thrills, spills, and drama, we can live out our lives through the rapid-fire series of images we see played out before our eyes. Your life may be boring and dull, but you can watch television and get some specious, voyeuristic thrill or satisfaction out of watching the lives of others. What else could explain the success of the various Big Brother franchises, where the boring lives of a bunch of freaky inadequates becomes compulsive viewing for millions? Is it simply the pharisaic buzz of "Lord, I thank you that I am not like other men" we get when watching these weirdos strut their stuff; or does the act of watching them have a strangely comforting and soporific effect on our own senses? Probably a bit of both. And TV's ability to juxtapose the serious with the stupid, and to reduce even the most complex discussions to a few simplistic sound bites shows just how difficult it is to convey anything either subtle or truly challenging. When TV becomes more than an occasional distraction, it becomes a soporific medium designed to dull the senses of its willing victims.

Of course, the need to be a commercial success and to have mass appeal virtually guarantees that TV will always tend to the lowest, blandest common cultural denominator. If something is radical and shocking, it will probably boost viewing figures for a short time; but then it rapidly ceases to be radical and shocking as it is slowly accommodated to the marketplace so that it can be sold to as many as possible; if there is no such accommodation, it will die the death of an unmarketable product. Homosexuality is the obvious example: how disturbing and anarchic is the homosexual impulse! Yet how comfy and middle class it has become in an era where virtually every interior designer on the TV is obviously gay. These people don't smash up society; they redecorate it with the help of some tasteful purchases from Pier 1 Imports.

This brings us to the bland aesthetics of the pop musicians of *American Idol*. Dare I say it? When a TV audience gets to choose the pop star, the result is scarcely going to be a Woody Guthrie or a Bob Dylan. Bland is going to rule the day. So, when Pope Benedict has Kelly Clarkson fronting him as his support band, he is co-opted by the blandness of the TV world and arguably jeopardizes any critical or prophetic edge he might have had. Indeed, this is just a microcosm of the whole visit: the whole thing was one huge TV event involving pilgrimages from one pop culture site and content to the next. But of course, the pope is only doing what Rome has done best through the years: adapting to the current cultural context. In times past, Rome would have replaced the god who looked after the village well with a patron saint, and thus Christianized villages without really challenging the underlying pagan values. Today, Pope Benedict speaks to young people after they have been "warmed up"—or should it be "put to sleep"—by one of the blandest and least-threatening phenomena of recent cultural history. In the words of Led Zeppelin (now that would have been a support band worth having), the singer changes, but the song remains the same. And every time, the really prophetic possibility of proclaiming Christ is lost in the soporific clouds of opium smoke in the surrounding culture.

It is a fine line between cultural contextualization and cultural syncretism. Rome has consistently blurred that boundary over the years and, to be honest, proved remarkably successful at it, from the substitution of the pagan pantheon with patron saints, to the triumph of Jesuit moral probabilism in seventeenth-century France, to hobnobbing with Muslim leaders, to the co-opting of *American Idol* for the latest world tour. Yet the problem is no less for us Protestants. Indeed, it should be greater, because orthodox Protestantism has traditionally been less willing on paper to allow a blurring of the boundary between the God of the Bible and the world around us; but, in our drive to be successful, there is still a constant temptation to judge our success by the criteria of the wider culture, to adopt the methods of the wider culture, and to co-opt the movers and shakers of the wider culture. We may not appear on stage with Ms. Clarkson, but that's probably because we haven't been invited, not because we are acting out of principle. And we have our own celebrity culture, our own conference groupies, our own ambitions to seize the modern media for Christ. In so doing, we surely underestimate the power of the modern media to consume and subvert all that touches it.

I saw the new James Bond movie over the weekend. Nothing like it to make me proud to be English. After all, it just couldn't be done by, say, the Welsh. "The name's ap-Llymrys Jones, Gwynfor ap-Llymrys Jones" just doesn't cut it frankly.

16

REFLECTIONS ON ROME PART I:
CONNECTING THE MIND
AND THE TONGUE

January 2010

I HAVE SPENT most of my life connected in some sense to Rome. At school and then at university, I was a Classics man. I preferred Greek tragedy to Roman comedy; but when it came to history, politics, poetry, and oratory, I was a Rome man. Julius Caesar, Vergil, and, above all, the great Cicero, were the figures who dominated my imagination. Then, as I moved beyond undergraduate studies into the field of Reformation history for my PhD, Rome was still dominant; not this time the machinations of the Senate, the declamations of Cicero, or the poetic escapades of Aeneas, but the Rome of Renaissance popes, papal bulls, and Tridentine Catholicism.

Yet, although I have spent barely a day in the last thirty years without thinking of Rome at some point, I had never actually set foot in the city until last month.

It is difficult to articulate the impact that walking into Vatican City and up the avenue to St. Peter's has on one's psyche. You can see all the photographs of it you want, as with the Grand Canyon, but when you are there, the real thing exists on an entirely different plane. As a European, I spent my childhood holidays running around large ancient buildings—Warwick Castle was a particular favorite—so I am not particularly impressed by size or age; but St. Peter's is on a different scale. As I turned the corner and came to the square, the colonnades seemed to be sweeping out to greet me like giant arms about to embrace the world, an intentional vision of Catholic aspirations, I am sure; and as I walked into the building itself, I was cowed into complete and awesome silence. The only other experience I have had that came remotely close was my first trip to New York when I stepped down from the coach and looked up—and up and up and up—at buildings that seemed almost to disappear into the sky. I felt small. And I felt even more so as I entered the great basilica at the heart of Vatican City. The scale of the place, the paintings, the beauty, the statues, the faces of popes gazing at me, the good, the bad, but not (at least as portrayed by the artists) particularly ugly.

The overwhelming power of the place pulled me in different directions. It was both terrifying and attractive. I suddenly realized why so many American evangelicals are attracted to the institution: it has everything American evangelicalism lacks—history, beauty, self-conscious identity, and, quite frankly, class. I also realized that such a vast organization simply does not need anybody else. Evangelicals may like to think of themselves as "dialogue partners" with Rome in certain contexts; but this is rather like Britain partnering with the U.S.A. in foreign policy adventures. Even those who have never heard of the Suez Crisis know who is really in charge. Indeed, the Vatican International Bookshop provided a symbolic example of the issue. It was there that I bought a copy of Benedict XVI's memoirs, a major part of which described his doctoral work on Bonaventure and its impact on his understanding of revelation and tradition. The only Protestant book I could find there was an Italian translation of Rick Warren on the Christmas story. I did not purchase that, even as a way of sharpening my Italian reading skills. Enough said.

The aesthetic sledgehammer of St. Peter's was impressive enough; but when you add to that the Vatican museum, along with the Sistine Chapel, the experience is one of aesthetic overload. From the pillars in the square to Michelangelo's depiction of creation and fall, the church in Rome projects an unequivocal message of beauty, power, and its own immensity in comparison with any and all pretenders.

But St. Peter's and the Vatican Museum were not my only points of call in the city. I also stopped by the great Gregorianum, the elite university where the most brilliant minds of the Jesuit Order are trained. The building was imposing; the library impressive; and the bookshop very serious: walls of biblical commentaries (many of them Protestant) and weighty tomes and textbooks of patristic theology, canon law, and philosophy, and of the greatest minds Catholicism has ever produced. No evangelical therapeutic psychobabble here, nor Rick Warren for that matter; indeed, I suspect he would have to be translated into Hungarian for his books to be deemed a sufficient intellectual challenge to make it into the inventory.

Now, let's pause for a second. I want to go on record at this point as saying that I understand the attraction of Rome: the sheer mass of the organization (if you'll pardon the pun); the overwhelming aesthetics; the desirability of belonging to such an august and ancient institution that knows what it is, where it comes from, and where it is going; and the cornucopia of brilliant intellects that have debated, refined, and articulated its confession over the centuries. All that I understand; all that I find attractive; all that I find superior to what evangelical Protestantism has to offer, particularly in its crassest megachurch and Emergent varieties. And, if asked whether I would rather spend an evening reading the typical evangelical offerings of my own tradition or some work by Aquinas or Newman or Kung or Ratzinger, I would be inclined to respond by inquiring as to whether such was a serious question. Against the background of the tweets, faceblogs, and submoronic inanity of the evangelical "here's a pic of me and my mate Kev" brigade, such is equivalent to asking me whether I would rather get tickets to hear Miley Cyrus or a Pink Floyd reunion. Catholic cathedrals—whether of stone or of intellect—have no real rivals, certainly not among megachurch maestros and Emergent egos.

But, having said all this, I find it hard to connect the mind—the Catholic mind—to the tongue. No, this is not some claim that Catholicism is just a bit too mystical for me, that it is so ineffable that it cannot be articulated in words; nor is it to suggest that Catholics gossip more than others, or speak before they think. Not at all. Let me explain. St. Peter's was not the only basilica I visited while in Italy. I also went to Padua and visited the famous Basilica of Saint Anthony. Again, the architecture, internal and external, was impressive; but most striking of all were the remains of St. Anthony of Padua himself.

Most of him is contained in a large and mercifully opaque sarcophagus; but three particular bits are on display in clear glass jars in one of the side chapels. To be precise, there you will find his lower jaw (with definite signs of the saint having endured British dentistry), his vocal chords (most pleasant), and his tongue (some things are best left unsaid). They are easy to spot, being right next to a piece of the true cross, also on display.

What can I say about the shows of devotion and veneration that I witnessed around these cadaverous morsels? Frankly, I found them repellent, little more than a manifestation of the crassest kind of superstitious folk religion. This is what is so difficult to connect with Catholicism of the von Balthasar or Yves Congar or De Lubac variety. Great and brilliant as these men were, at ground level Catholicism looks like benighted old biddies doing homage before an amputated and pickled tongue. It does not matter how many American evangelical leaders are wined and dined by the Roman See, or are taken by some cardinal to gaze upon *Codex Sinaiticus*, the tongue and its accoutrements remain as a silent testimony to superstition, as much a reflection of the priorities of the hierarchy as the mandatory polyglottic competence of the students—the students! not just the lecturers—at places such as the Gregorianum.

Of course, one response is that all churches have their areas of nuttiness, corruption, and superstition. This is true; Protestantism has its Benny Hinns, for sure, although one of the great things about denominations is that one can distance oneself somewhat from the loonies—or at least choose the loonies with whom one wishes to fraternize. And no Protestant should ever try to play holier than thou with a Catholic on the church's record on sexual morality. Even in my limited ecclesiastical experience, I've come across adultery, rape, and child abuse within orthodox Reformed circles, and seen attempts by church leaders to sweep the same under the rug. But it is one thing to have the odd loony or the occasional bit of wackiness or sleaze; it is quite another to promote such as good for the church and, indeed, to make it an integral part of one's piety. Yet this is what is done with St. Anthony's tongue and with other bits of his anatomy. Equally dubious—and central—are figures such as Padre Pio, the miracle worker and stigmatic who, in 2006, was voted the person to whom Italian Catholics most often prayed. There is something surely wrong when Jesus doesn't make the top three in such a poll, and the church does not take immediate and significant remedial action.

Since visiting St. Anthony's, I have tried my best through reading the right Catholic sources and talking to good Catholic friends to understand what is going on in a church that embraces the most brilliant theology and the most crass superstition; and that not simply in the way that the church should embrace the good and the bad, but as an integral part of her identity and outreach. Thus far, I have drawn a blank. I was particularly disappointed by Hans Kung. Kung usually does a better hatchet job on his own church than the fiercest Protestant bigot; but on Padre Pio and his ilk, I found him sadly lacking. In his memoirs he recalls visiting Pio in the 1950s at his mother's request, because his brother was dying of cancer. His comments in that passage on Pio, and on Lourdes, seem to suggest that he sees their value in the fact that they give people something in which to believe; that such belief has benefits; and thus the whole paraphernalia that these things represent is good. Pragmatism; pure pragmatism in a liberal Catholic idiom.

I close with three thoughts. First, my trip to Rome reminded me once again of how inadequate evangelical Protestant literature on contemporary Catholicism is. It tends to be either of the "Vatican II changed nothing and the pope is still Antichrist" variety, or the equally unhelpful and inaccurate "Vatican II changed everything and, frankly, I cannot remember why I am still a Protestant" kind. We need some good Protestant writing on this subject that will help future pastors, elders, and church members engage thoughtfully, respectfully, and in an informed manner, with Catholicism and Catholic friends.

Second, I was challenged by a Catholic friend, when I raised the issues of Padre Pio and St. Anthony's tongue, to consider whether my own reaction was conditioned in part by my being more a son of David Hume and the Enlightenment than I care to admit. Easy to dismiss this point, but it perhaps deserves more reflection than I have given it. There is a fine line between credulity and skepticism; and I am mindful of that statement by Newman in his work on the Arian controversy: "[H]e who believes a little, but encompasses that little with the inventions of men, is undeniably in a better condition than he who blots out from his mind both the human inventions, and that portion of truth that was concealed in them."[1] A biblical balance is needed; and I am not sure that I have necessarily found it myself.

1. John Henry Newman, *The Arians of the Fourth Century* (London: Longmans, Green and Co., 1901), 85.

Finally, it seems that it is very easy for American Catholic intellectuals, and those evangelicals who are attracted by Rome, to ignore the tongues, the jaws, the bits of the real cross, the stigmatics, the folk religion. But American pick-n-mix consumerism applied to Catholicism is just one more manifestation of—dare I say it?—the modern Western aesthetic of choice; it is emphatically not the same as Catholicism as it works itself out in the very backyard of the Roman See; and it will not do simply to say that the practices of such are not significant; they are significant, at least for anyone who takes seriously their Catholicism. The picture in Rome, in Padua, in San Giovanni Rotondo, is more complicated than Evangelicals and Catholics Together, and those evangelicals and would-be converts who would put down the *Codex Sinaiticus* and step outside the precincts of the Vatican to observe what goes on in Italy in the name of the church might find their excitement at meeting with a cardinal or two somewhat tempered by silent tongues that have long since ceased wagging but that continue to speak eloquently about certain priorities in Catholicism.

Just received the two latest tracts by Jack Chick. Relevant, sensitive, and scrupulously accurate as always, these are on Islam. Two things are worthy of note: first, the wonderfully ethnically sensitive portrayal of the physiognomy of Arabs. Mmmm, where have I seen pics like this before? Oohh, yes, I remember—some ten years ago when I was researching a paper on Luther and the Jews and spent the day in Cambridge University Library looking at German propaganda cartoons about the Jews from the 1930s and 1940s. Who says the church can't learn from Goebbels?

Second, I learned that Khadijah, the Prophet's first wife, was—you guessed it—a Catholic! So, by clear implication, Islam is—right again!—a Catholic conspiracy!!!! As usual, only Jack has the courage to tell it as it really is. And I thought it was the Welsh who were to blame! Now I don't need to feel a sense of national guilt anymore. I feel so happy. (Me too—Del Boy)

I do recommend these tracts for Catholic, Muslim, and Welsh friends—they'll love them and find Christianity a really attractive prospect. Anyway, must dash—the senior nurse is coming round to secure me in my straitjacket and padded cell for the night and she'll kill me if she finds me blogging.

17

REFLECTIONS ON ROME PART II: THE NEED FOR HISTORY 101

March 2010

IN THE PREVIOUS CHAPTER, I reflected on my experience in Rome and Padua shortly before Christmas of 2009, a week that involved the awesome beauty of the Vatican, the dazzling intellectual accomplishments of Catholic theological education, and the weird folk religion that surrounds relics such as the tongue of St. Anthony of Padua.

Between wandering around spectacular pieces of art, paying homage at the bust of Cicero (which, much to my chagrin, I discovered might not be Cicero after all), and eating some of the best food I have ever tasted, I did get a chance or two to do some actual work. Perhaps the most unusual opportunity was the invitation to present a seminar on "Giovanni Calvino" at the Diocese of Trento's Interfaith Dialogue Centre.

Trento, of course, was the place where the famous Council took place in the sixteenth century, not merely defining Catholicism in a clearer and more comprehensive way than ever before, but also helping to trigger the great era of Protestant confessionalization, as Europe's territories sought to give theological expression to their emerging identities. I spent a couple of hours wandering around the city, still beautifully and distinctly medieval in appearance, and also touring the cathedral. Unlike St. Peter's in Rome, this was a dark building, and somewhat claustrophobic, easily tempting the Protestant visitor to draw metaphysical conclusions from what was really just a typical facet of a certain type of medieval architecture.

The seminar went well. The priest in charge was a delightful fellow who made me and my Protestant companions most welcome. A brief perusal of the books in his study indicated that confessional Protestantism rated somewhat lower than Buddhism on the reading list priorities, but I was genuinely honored and delighted to be given an opportunity to speak in such a setting.

The content of my seminar was straightforward enough: a brief outline of Calvin's life; and then discussion of both his exegetical techniques and the theological underpinnings of his thought. I had chosen these topics for a purpose: each allowed me to connect Calvin to both patristic and medieval antecedents, and thus provided a point of contact with the tradition of my Catholic hosts.

The Catholics in the audience did not respond to my points about Calvin's exegesis, but one thoughtful priest did pick up on the late-medieval context I had drawn, arguing that the Scotism that underlies certain aspects of Calvin's thought inevitably led to radical skepticism. I won't delay *Ref21* readers by elaborating the thesis, but it harks back to the arguments laid out in the 1940s by a Catholic scholar, Joseph Lortz, who saw the Reformation as the result of a decadent and degenerate late-medieval theology that had abandoned the more faithfully Catholic paths laid out by Thomas Aquinas. On that one, you pay your money and take your choice; although my own work on later Reformed theologians such as John Owen has provided evidence that Thomism remained a force even within Protestantism.

What was surprising, however, was the number of questions I had to answer on the idea of Calvin as theocrat and as the murderer of Servetus. The former was easy to dispatch, as the late date of Calvin's citizenship in Geneva puts the lie to any notion that he was a Christian equivalent of an Iranian mullah. The Servetus questions, however, puzzled me; and I was sorely tempted to respond simply by pointing out that when it comes to blood on the church walls, Rome should probably not ask too many questions about the sixteenth and seventeenth centuries. Nevertheless, I offered a patient and detailed account of Servetus's life, of his involvement with both Catholics and Protestants, and of the certainty of his death at the hands of whoever reached him first. The smiles told me that I had probably not convinced everyone; but I had done my best.

The odd historiography of Protestantism that came through so clearly in the seminar in Trent resurfaced a few days later, on a flight from Rome to Padua. Flying Ryanair (no, that wasn't the enjoyable part, although it wasn't bad either—they don't yet charge you to use the toilet on the plane, despite the rumors), I found myself seated by a young guy in jeans and sweater who had escorted a group of nuns on board. We struck up a conversation, and it turned out that he was a priest in the Maronite Order who was taking his cousin and some sisters from her convent to Venice for the weekend to celebrate her successful completion of a PhD. When he asked what I did, and I told him I was a Presbyterian minister and a professor at a Protestant seminary, his eyes lit up, and what could have been a boring flight turned into a delightful conversation. Among other things, I learned that Maronite priests can marry—but he could not, because he had taken monastic vows; I also listened as he told me of growing up on the streets of Beirut in the 1980s, and how he had been injured when a rocket exploded while he played football; and I was moved as he informed me that he gave money to an evangelical mission in Turkey and prayed for the Protestants there.

In return, I told him of growing up in Gloucestershire—no bombs, only cheese rolling, which is nearly as dangerous and just as frightening; I also explained my academic research to him, how I had nerdishly spent much of my adult life examining the connection of medieval thought to Protestant orthodoxy. He seemed genuinely fascinated, although as an ice breaker at parties, I don't generally recommend the line "Do you think Scotus was right to deny the real distinction between existence and essence?" However, it soon became clear that his knowledge of Protestantism, and of the medieval scholastic traditions of Thomism and Scotism, was minimal. When we came to the Reformation, he was unaware that Luther had a sense of humor, a sure sign that his theological education had never required him to read Luther.

It is self-serving for a church historian to say this—although being self-serving does not make it any less true—that a knowledge of Catholicism is vital for Protestants, and vice versa. The theological and ecclesiastical upheavals of the sixteenth and seventeenth centuries, shaped as they undoubtedly were by wider factors such as economic, cultural, and political changes, are central to what both Catholicism and Protestantism became. Catholicism is not simply Protestantism with different doctrines; while we share a common grounding in Nicea and Chalcedon, the two faiths have differing views of authority, of the sacraments, of the nature and function of faith, and of the nature of the church. In an era that oscillates between neglecting history and simply regarding history as something negative or oppressive, it is easy to lose sight of the significance of these differences and reduce them to Swift's Lilliputian struggles over which end of a boiled egg should be removed at the breakfast table; or to misunderstand the differences completely, and, as with the gentle priest who chaired my seminar in Trento, see them as purely matters of seditious individual ambition and the abuse of religious power. Only a careful, articulate education in the history of Catholicism will help Protestants truly to understand it and, where necessary, argue against it; and the same holds true for Catholics. We cannot even agree to differ with any integrity if we have not taken the time to learn each other's history.

As I disembarked at Padua Airport, my newfound priest friend turned to me. "How long are you staying in Venice?" he asked. "I'm not," I replied, my disappointment anticipating the invitation to come. "I teach today and then head back to Trento tonight." "What a pity," he declared. "The nuns will all be in bed by 8 and I was hoping we could continue our conversation over a drink. No one should be in bed by 8 o'clock in Venice." On that, we could both agree.

18

Beyond the Limitations of Chick Lit

May 2007

A FRIEND RECENTLY asked me to put down a few reflections on Roman Catholicism, whether I thought it was on the whole a good thing or a bad thing. The conversion of Francis Beckwith, the ETS president, to Roman Catholicism has perhaps made the subject of more immediate relevance than might otherwise have been the case. So, for what they are worth, here are my thoughts. In this article, I offer a few areas where Protestants can learn from Catholics, or share common ground; next, I will offer a few areas where Protestants necessarily diverge from Catholicism.

I should preface the following by noting first that there is not much good confessional Protestant interaction available in print that deals with post-Vatican II Catholicism. Boettner's pre-Vatican II work, a classic of its kind, is out of date; Berkouwer's account of Vatican II is fascinating but flavored by the theology of his own later years; and, a few interesting collections of essays notwithstanding, there is no really scholarly critique of Vatican II Catholicism from an evangelical perspective.

As a general piece of advice, however, it is worth avoiding "Chick lit"—no, I am not saying that it is always a mistake to pass a Catholic friend a copy of *Bridget Jones's Diary* or something on the Ya-Ya Sisterhood; rather, I am thinking of the graphic novellas of the venerable Jack Chick, fixated as they are on an evil and conspiratorial Rome, which are not to my mind the best resource for developing an understanding of contemporary Catholicism or for interacting with Catholic friends. The Chick tracts are replete with unpleasantness: the "cookie god," cartoons of ethnic stereotypes worthy of Julius Streicher, and disturbing images of pregnant ladies being tortured by medieval Inquisitors in quasi-Klan garb. These do tell the reader quite a lot about something but not, I suspect, about contemporary Roman Catholicism. Contra Chick lit and popular Protestant shibboleths, there are numerous aspects of Catholicism that should resonate with thoughtful Protestants and that we neglect to our own impoverishment.

Quality Christian Writing

The first is, perhaps, one that is not always noted by those who think in strictly theological categories: Catholicism has produced the most stimulating literary figures of the Christian tradition, broadly considered. First, there is the incomparable G. K. Chesterton. Humor and irony in the service of theology? Can a Protestant do that? Well, Luther would have approved of the idea; it's there at the very inception of the Protestant tradition, and it is a great shame we have lost it. If you want to know how much we have lost, then spend a few hours perusing the works of Chesterton, who does for basic creedal Christianity what Terry Eagleton does for Marxist literary criticism.

Then for anyone wanting to wrestle with issues of evil and redemption, is there a better novel than *Brighton Rock* by Graham Greene? And to this one can add the names of Walker Percy, Flannery O'Connor, Evelyn Waugh, and (at least arguably—I know scholars divide on the issue) William Shakespeare. Tolkien too— although, as a loyal English Brummy, I tend to claim him geographically for the Midlands, rather than theologically for the church. All of these writers offer literary expressions of various grand moral and theological themes with which Protestants should be able to resonate. Indeed, as a good Calvinist, I find myself more in agreement with Greene's take on human nature than I do with the sort of Pelagian tosh one finds in most Christian bookshops.

A Shared Creedal Tradition of Trinitarianism

The second area is that of the creeds. Here, Catholics and confessional Protestants share a high regard for the great ecumenical statements of the early church, particularly the Nicene-Constantinopolitan Creed, the Apostles' Creed, and the Athanasian Creed. Indeed, given the fact that the Christian God is not just any god in general but a very particular God—the one who is three in one, Father, Son, and Holy Spirit—this common Trinitarian ground epitomized in the Nicene Creed is no small thing. Ironically, the explicit presence of this in the Catholic liturgy guarantees the obvious Trinitarian aspect of Christian worship; while much evangelical Protestantism repudiates use of creeds in worship out of a desire to be more scriptural, yet fails to offer any adequate alternative for safeguarding the Trinity in worship—and thus the explicitly Christian nature of the God being worshiped. As evangelical Protestants, we should humbly acknowledge our common Trinitarian heritage with the Catholic Church and make our criticisms of their liturgy on this point not by shouting the odds about the Scripture principle vis-à-vis use of man-made creeds in worship (most Protestants use hymnbooks, not psalters after all!) but by showing them a better way, if indeed there is such.

Great Christian Theologians

The third area where Protestants should appreciate Catholicism is that of certain great theologians. Of course, it should go without saying that the early church fathers who provided the intellectual and theological background to the creeds should be part of any Protestant minister's or teacher's education, along with obvious later authors such as Augustine, without whom neither traditional Catholicism nor confessional Protestantism can possibly be understood.

But there are other, more definitely Catholic authors with whom every thoughtful, theological Protestant should be familiar. Thomas Aquinas is one, partly because he is without doubt the single most important intellectual source for pre-Vatican II Catholicism, but also partly because his writings represent a classic statement and defense of some basic doctrines that, say, Catholicism and Reformed Protestantism hold in common. For example, he is anti-Pelagian, and his basic statement of the doctrine of God forms the foundation for later Reformed Orthodox notions of the same, critically appropriated through a later exegetical and philosophical grid. In my own studies of John Owen, I soon discovered that to understand the mind of the great Puritan I first had to understand the mind of the Angelic Doctor.

148

Yet no Protestant reading list should end with Aquinas. The writings of Blaise Pascal are also a treasure trove: his *Provincial Letters* is perhaps the single greatest piece of satirical religious polemic ever produced, a devastating critique of both semi-Pelagianism and theological verbiage with which all Christian leaders should acquaint themselves. And as for his *Thoughts*, there is so much gold to be mined from his thought-provoking reflections on life and culture that these aphorisms are probably more relevant now than the day he penned them. Pascal sees through the superficiality of a culture obsessed with pleasure and busy-ness in a manner more devastating and astute than any other theologian with whom I am acquainted.

One could go on: from John Henry Newman to Etienne Gilson down to figures such as Brian Davies and Thomas Weinandy in our own day, the Catholic Church has produced a stream of outstanding theological writers who are worth reading; even at those points where the Protestant reader must part company with them, the stimulation to clarity of thought they offer is worth its weight in gold. Indeed, I would argue there are few greater prose stylists in English literature seen as a whole than the great Cardinal Newman, a master wordsmith. As for contemporary theology, I have for many years preferred to read the latest thoughtful Catholic writers than their often all-too-superficial evangelical contemporaries. To listen to a Catholic like Eugene McCarraher on, say, postmodernism is far more stimulating, critically profound, and thought provoking than any post-evangelical with whom I am acquainted.

Common Cause on Moral Issues

A fourth area where Protestants can stand profitably with Catholics is that of moral issues. Many of the current moral challenges that concern Protestants—abortion, gay marriage, poverty, social justice—are areas where there is a strong tradition of Catholic reflection and practice that can be studied with profit by Protestants. Abortion, right to life issues, and human sexuality are all areas where Catholicism and Protestantism share common ground; and the numerical strength, media savvy, and political power of the Catholic Church ensures these issues have a higher public profile than might otherwise be the case. It is worth injecting the caveat that on some of these matters the foundations of Catholic thought are not shared by Protestantism. For example, opposition to homosexual marriage is predicated at least in part on the fact that such marriage breaks the link between sexual intercourse and reproduction. Most Protestants (and Catholics!) already break this link through the use of contraception, and thus many Catholic thinkers would regard Protestant opposition to homosexuality as fatally compromised at the outset. Nevertheless, in the public square the practical policies desired by conservative Catholics and conservative Protestants are substantially the same.

Church Loyalty

A fifth area of positive note, and one where Protestants can really learn from Catholics, is church loyalty. For all of the concerns I have about Catholic notions of the church and of worship, there is one thing I find remarkable and impressive: the loyalty of many Catholics to the church and not to particular personalities. So often in Protestantism the attitude toward the church as an institution is weak or nonexistent. Thus, a Protestant church calls a pastor whom some of the congregation do not like because they find his preaching boring or his family difficult or his way of running congregational meetings to be less than stellar; the reaction of many of those less than satisfied with their new minister is simply to resign their membership and move on to the next church—and to keep moving until they find a church that meets all their needs. What I find striking about Catholic friends is that the arrival of a priest with whom they are less than enamored rarely leads them to move on in this fashion. The local church is not treated as lightly as many Protestants treat theirs. Now, I am of course aware that some of the reasons for this difference in response are in theory theological; but in practice I suspect that Protestant wanderings are rather more to do with allowing taste to trump ecclesiology than with real issues of substantial principle. The ecclesiological loyalty of Catholics may be theologically misplaced; but the response to that is for Protestants to do better, not abandon ecclesiology wholesale as is so often the case.

These, then, are five areas where I believe Protestants can fruitfully learn from Catholicism.

I now want to spend my time looking at areas where principled disagreements exist. I hope I do this not with a censorious or pharisaic spirit, but out of a desire that there are points where Protestants and Catholics must part company because of sincerely held, cherished beliefs. Of course, these areas of disagreement are often historically and theologically complex, and cannot be dealt with in any truly adequate way here; so what I offer is, in effect, a short inventory of such that I hope will act as a starting point for further investigation and reflection.

Tradition and Authority

Ask a thoughtful Protestant about where Protestantism and Catholicism most significantly diverge, and it is likely that he will mention the closely related areas of tradition and authority. Now, Protestants tend to be very suspicious of any talk of tradition as playing a role in theology, as it would seem to stand somewhat in tension with the Reformation's view of Scripture alone as the authoritative basis for theological reflection. In fact, the Reformation itself represented a struggle over two types of tradition, that which scholars call T1, tradition based on Scripture as the sole source of revelation (the position of Protestants such as Luther and Calvin, and of some pre-Tridentine Catholics), and that which they term T2, tradition based on two sources, namely, Scripture and an oral tradition mediated through the teaching magisterium of the church. This latter was arguably the position codified at the Council of Trent, although it would seem that the boundary between T1 and T2 is in practice often blurred, and very difficult to define in any formal or precise sense; nevertheless, as a heuristic device the distinction is useful, and it is really only as Protestants come to understand exactly what is the Catholic view of tradition (i.e., T1 plus T2) that they can come to properly understand how tradition (T1) does not subvert the notion of Scripture alone.

A moment's reflection on Protestant practice should demonstrate the truth of this. Every time a Protestant minister takes a commentary off his shelf to help with sermon preparation, or opens a volume of systematic theology, or attends a lecture on a theological topic, he practically acknowledges the importance of T1, whether he cares to admit it or no. A belief in Scripture as a unique and all-sufficient cognitive foundation for theology does not, indeed, cannot, preclude the use of extrabiblical and thus traditional sources for help. Protestantism and Catholicism both value tradition; the difference lies in the source and authority of this tradition: Protestant tradition is justified by, and is ultimately only binding insofar as it represents a synthesis of the teaching of the one normative source of revelation, holy Scripture.

Catholicism is more flexible. Although, as noted above, the boundary where T1 ends and T2 begins is not an easy one to formalize or define, Catholicism has proved far more open to the development of dogmas not immediately justifiable on the basis of Scripture, and has also been willing to take more seriously ancient practice as a significant guide. Thus, the practice of praying to saints has no apparent scriptural warrant, but was something evident very early on in the postapostolic era, a point used by Catholics to argue for its validity (a good example of a T2 dogma).

The difference on tradition, of course, connects to other differences on authority. Undergirding Protestant notions of Scripture is a belief in the basic perspicuity of the Christian message. This lay at the heart of Luther's dispute with Erasmus. Erasmus saw Scripture as complicated and obscure and thus as requiring the teaching magisterium of the church to give definitive explanations of what it teaches; Luther saw the basic message as clear and accessible to all who had eyes to see and ears to hear. The basic Erasmus-Luther dispute epitomizes the Catholic-Protestant divide on this issue and also reminds us of why the papacy and the teaching magisterium of the church are so crucial in Catholicism. The problem of the Anglican, John Henry Newman, as he wrote his masterpiece on the development of doctrine, was not that doctrine developed, but how Protestantism could discern which developments were legitimate and which were not. By the time the work was published, Newman was a Catholic, having become convinced that the authority of Rome, not the scriptural perspicuity of Wittenberg, was the only means to resolve the problem.

One might add here, almost as an aside, that the canonical and hermeneutical chaos of modern Protestant biblical studies and systematic theology, along with the moral and epistemological and ecclesiological anarchy it brings in its wake, is inherently unstable from an ecclesiastical perspective. It is surely not surprising that it has provided the context for some high-profile conversions to Rome over recent decades: Protestantism was born out of convictions regarding Scripture's basic perspicuity; the destruction of that doctrine can be read as an unwitting *prolegomenon* to a return to an authority structure that is functionally like that of Rome; and, given the choice of scholars or postmodern *arrivistes* or the vicar of Rome calling the shots, it is not surprising that many have chosen the latter. The New Perspective on Paul is the most obvious attack on Luther's legacy in Protestantism; but just as significant is so much of modern hermeneutics, representing as it does the posthumous triumph of the spirit of Erasmus over that of Luther.

Other Religions

One of the great mysteries for casual observers of Catholicism since the 1970s has been the apparent conflict between internal and external Vatican policies. On the one hand, liberal Catholic teachers such as Kung and Schillebeeckx have found themselves on the receiving end of very conservative internal reforms; on the other hand, both John Paul II and Benedict XVI have pursued what seem to be (from an evangelical Protestant perspective) a fairly liberal and concessive attitude toward other religions, most notably Islam.

Vatican policy is, in fact, consistent with Vatican beliefs, despite the appearance. The Catholic catechism is clear that the God of Christianity and the God of, say, Islam, are the same God. This does not relativize Catholicism and Islam in terms of making them equally legitimate expressions of human worship, but it does reflect the standard Catholic acknowledgment of Christianity as a higher and purer form of the more general phenomenon of theism. Now, natural theology is a vexed issue in Protestantism, partly because of Karl Barth's belligerent "NO!" to Emil Brunner in the 1930s, and partly because of the persistent misreading of the Reformers and the Reformed Orthodox on these issues through the popular historiography of the issue at the hands of writers as diverse as Francis Schaeffer, Cornelius Van Til, and Stanley Grenz and their various disciples. Yet even the most historically sensitive reading of confessional Protestant traditions requires us to emphasize the centrality of the Trinity to divine identity and revelation, and to use this as a critical measure by which to judge other religions, such as Islam. For a confessional Protestant, if Allah is one, if Allah has no Son, then Allah is not Jehovah, for Jehovah is not god in general but God the Triune in particular; consequently, there should be no joint worship services with the local imam, no blurring of the religious boundaries, whatever popular-front platforms we might share on moral issues.

Sacraments, Justification, and Assurance

The most obvious aesthetic difference between Catholicism and Protestantism is the role of sacraments, specifically that of the Mass or the Lord's Supper, in the respective traditions. Walk into Cologne Cathedral and your eyes are immediately drawn to the far end of the aisle, where the altar stands; walk into St. Giles's Cathedral, Edinburgh, and your eyes are drawn to the center, where the pulpit stands. The respective architects knew their theology, as each building focuses attention on the most important action that takes place there. While Catholics have always had preaching, they focus on the Mass; while Protestants have always had sacraments, they focus on the reading and preaching of the Word.

Underlying these differences of emphasis are basic differences of theology. Catholics see grace as coming through sacramental participation in the church; Protestants see grace as coming to them through the promise of the Word grasped by faith as it is read and preached. Then, allied to these differences are others: Catholicism sees justification as a process whereby the righteousness of Christ is imparted to the believer through this sacramental participation; Reformation Protestantism sees the righteousness of Christ as imputed to the believer by grace through faith in Christ. Catholicism understands human nature in terms of substance; Protestantism understands it in terms of relation. Salvation for Catholics thus involves a substantial change; for Protestantism, it involves a change in relation or status.

Much has been written, of course, about the basic agreement between Catholicism and Protestantism on justification, but the differences listed above are real and cannot be sidelined as minor aberrations. Post-Christian feminist Daphne Hampson has written of the failure of ecumenical discussions to address seriously the fundamental differences on human identity, and I find myself in basic agreement with her on this point. One could go further: the continuing centrality of the Mass, the persistence of Catholic catechetical belief in purgatory, and the Tridentine emphasis on

human ability vis-à-vis grace, all show that there remain fundamental differences between Rome and Geneva on this issue. We
share a common Pauline canon and vocabulary, and we share a
history of Augustinian conceptualization of issues surrounding
matters of grace and salvation, but we can only unite if one, or
both, of the sides abandon(s) cherished beliefs that lie at the heart
of our respective theological and ecclesiastical identities.

Now, many Protestants cannot articulate a full-blown doctrine
of justification by grace through faith, in much the same way as many
Catholics do not really understand the Mass. We can be thankful we
are not saved by commitment to a dogma but by believing in Jesus
Christ. But the difference on justification leads to a fundamentally
different view of the Christian life. For the Catholic, assurance of
God's favor is a non-issue; indeed, assurance can be a dangerously
subversive thing, encouraging moral laxity and poor churchman-
ship. For the Protestant, however, it is absolutely crucial: only as we
are assured of God's favor can we understand his holiness without
despairing, and do good works—live as Christians!—in a manner
that is not servile but rather affiliative and familial. Catholics and,
indeed, Protestants who have a faulty understanding of justification, are at the very least losing out on the sheer joy and delight of
the assured Christian life.

I hope these few brief thoughts have highlighted some areas
of disagreement between Catholicism and Protestantism. I am a
committed, passionate Protestant; but I can recognize in Catholicism much in which I take delight even as I see much from which I
must differ. I have said it before in this column and I will say it again:
Protestants need good reasons not to be Catholic. Catholicism is the
Western default position. If you do not regard the great confessions

and catechisms of the sixteenth and seventeenth centuries as being biblical in their teaching on justification, then you should probably do the decent thing and become a Catholic. The implications your position has for Scripture's teaching, for church history, and for notions of authority, makes such a move a good one. Converting to Catholicism is not a crime, after all. Yet justification is not the only issue: if you buy into the theological anarchy of modern evangelical thought, then acknowledge it for what it is—a statement about the fundamental obscurity of Scripture's teaching—and do what Newman did in similar circumstances: turn to Rome.

If, however, you value the Protestant tradition on justification, and its concomitant pastoral point, that of the normativity of the individual's assurance, you may, indeed, you should, appreciate much of what Catholicism and Protestantism share in common, but you should remain at Geneva and not head to Rome. For me, the right to claim Question One of the Heidelberg Catechism as my own, as the most profound statement of a truly childlike faith and ethic, is too precious to cede either to the numpties of postmodern evangelicalism or the geniuses of Rome, even the great Newman:

Question: What is your only comfort in life and death?

Answer: That I with body and soul, both in life and death, am not my own, but belong unto my faithful saviour Jesus Christ who, with his precious blood, has fully satisfied for all my sins, and delivered me from all the power of the Devil; and so preserves me that without the will of my heavenly Father not a hair can fall from my head; yea, that all things must be subservient to my salvation, and, therefore, by his Holy Spirit, He also assures me of eternal life, and makes me sincerely willing, and ready, henceforth, to live unto him.

19

No Text, Please; I'm British!

February 2009

DESPITE THE RUMORS, I am not a technophobe. True, I am no good at technology; but I do not particularly fear it, as I might fear, say, the revival of disco music as a popular cultural phenomenon or a government-enforced William Shatner season on Turner Classic Movies. Thus, I love my computer; I just have no interest in using it for anything beyond writing, e-mailing, and the occasional Internet purchase. Fortunate to have a secretary who does the technological bits for me, I have neither need nor desire to master any further aspects of the technoworld. Indeed, I take some perverse pride in the fact that I can type with only one finger on each hand, romantically seeing this lack of polish as making me the modern equivalent of the 1930s hack journalist, cigarette hanging from the corner of his mouth, glass of bourbon on the bedside table, hammering out copy on an old typewriter in a dingy motel room.

Nevertheless, I did indulge in one journey into the virtual social world for a month or two just to see what, if anything, I was missing.

159

Late in the summer, I received an e-mail from a good friend, inviting me to sign up to an Internet professional network. This I did, typing in a minimum of personal information; then I sat back and waited. By the time I canceled my account in late December I had, I think, the grand total of seven contacts. This fact alone made me suspicious, as in real life I have only three friends. To be honest, I did nothing beyond accept invitations from others to link up; but then I started to get invitations to link up with people I did not know, hardly knew, or knew but with whom I didn't want to connect; at the same time, I did not want to cause offense by a refusal. So I closed my account and returned to the oblivion of the "Billy no virtual mates" milieu from which I had only recently escaped. The ethical dilemma of "to link or not to link" was thus definitively solved.

Now, I am basically a private person. Teaching and writing are my job, not my life; real life I reserve for family and church. As Bob Dylan sang in "Hurricane," "It's my work he'd say, I do it for pay, and when it's all over, just as soon be on my way." Outside of work, therefore, I have a small circle of close friends and otherwise keep myself to myself. Indeed, my wife would go so far as to tell you there are only two kinds of people I generally avoid: those I know and those I don't know. I don't even have an answering machine on my home phone, not because I think they are inherently evil, but because I have no use for one. I take the view that if someone really wants to contact me, they'll phone again; if they don't phone again, then it couldn't have been that important.

All this makes the whole idea of these Internet networking things, like personal blogs and Facebook and MySpace, a naturally somewhat alien phenomenon to me. After all, why would I want to parade the details of my life before the world? And why would I want to pretend to be friends with, or connected to, people I either do not like or have never met? Yet these web networking phenomena are exactly that: phenomena, remarkable in their power and their reach. For example, I recently heard from my mother in England that my eldest son has a girlfriend. How did an elderly English lady living in a tiny village in the West Country of England learn this detail of the emotional life of my Philadelphia-based son, something he had successfully concealed even from my panoptical wife? Well, my niece had seen it on his Facebook page and she had told my mother who then happened to mention it to me, assuming that I knew already. What an amazing world, where someone half a world away has access to domestic information about my household unknown even to myself.

Yet, while they may be phenomena, I am not sure that the success of things like Facebook, texting, etc. is entirely to be welcomed. True, there are advantages: for example, families and friends living at a distance can exchange photos and news with ease; but a touch of skepticism about these wonderful new web services is perhaps overdue.

For example, take the language of "friend." The way of connecting with people on Facebook is, apparently, to "friend" somebody. That the noun has become a verb is scarcely cause for concern; but the cheapening of the word surely is. Simply to be linked to someone on the Internet is not true friendship; yet the use of the word creates the image that such is the case, or at least blurs the difference between casual Internet acquaintance and somebody for whom one might have real affinity, affection, and concern. Our language should make it clear that textual intercourse on Facebook or the like is not to be considered true friendship, any more than viewing Internet pornography is to be considered true lovemaking.

Further, as the language of friendship is hijacked and cheapened by these Internet social networks, this cheapening itself is part and parcel of a redefining of intimacy based on the erosion of the boundaries between the public and private. Self-obsessed exhibitionist celebrities have for many years had the option of the Oprah-style chat-show, where they can parade their dirty laundry for all to see; lowlifes have had Jerry Springer and *Big Brother* and a myriad of "reality TV" shows; but now, with blogs and social network pages, any people with a computer can continuously flaunt their private lives and conversations, from the boring and trivial to the weird and perverted, for a potentially countless (and faceless) multitude to see.

Now, notions of privacy have always been fluid; but we stand at a point in history where the private could be potentially abolished in its entirety. Satellites allow anyone on the Internet to observe our houses; and pornography has mainstreamed to the point where, according to a recent article in *Business Week*, even Playboy is under huge financial pressure, being squeezed because equivalents of its soft-core product are available in ordinary weeklies, and it is simply too tame to compete with the hard-core material on the Internet. Many Christians would see this latter as the triumph of lust, and so it is; but is it not also a function of the dismantling of the notion of privacy whereby everything can and should be paraded for public consumption? Might it be that chat-show confessionals, navel-gazing personal blogs, and virtual social networks possibly stand in continuity with pornography, being functions of the same exhibitionist drive that dismantles decency by collapsing the public and the private?

More significant, however, is not so much the con game of false intimacy but the childishness that such language then encourages. As friendship is cheapened, so it begins to lose connection with adulthood. This is best seen in the negative. Last year, my then-secretary came to work one day, burst out laughing, and told me that somebody on Facebook had removed her and her husband as "friends." Oh my! What was she meant to do? Beg to be let back in? Immolate herself on the seminary lawn as an act of atonement? The terminology made the move seem ridiculously childish. Indeed, it reminded me of nothing so much as those times many years ago when my younger sisters would come home from primary school to tell my mother that they had stopped being friends with Jenny or Mary or Louise, because of some perceived slight inflicted by the (now former) friend. You can just imagine the kind of scene that caused such reaction: one girl excludes another from a game of hopscotch as part of a puerile playground power play, provoking the retort, "I'm not going to be your friend, so there!" Just the kind of idiom, honed to perfection in the playground bitchiness of prepubescent girls, that the terminology of Facebook seems to have universalized across the age barriers of the real world. The language of Facebook both reflects and encourages childishness; indeed, judging by the tantrums, spitefulness, and cowardly rants on many blogs and web pages, childishness has become something of a textually transmitted disease.

So where is all this leading? I want to suggest that one of the key problems with Internet friendships, with texting, with blogs, etc., is the lack of the body in the means of communication and relationship. The elimination of bodily interaction on the web is not significant only in the realm of sex and pornography. Think about it: virtual relationships of all kinds, not simply the sexual, inevitably lack depth and nuance. When I speak to my wife, or one of my friends, the tone of voice, the look on my face, the touch of my hand, the million and one unconscious physical "tells" communicate to the person as much, if not more, than the words I speak. Mature, deep, meaningful friendships involve the ability of both parties to read and understand each other in ways that enrich and often transcend the words that are spoken. Even the telephone allows for some nuance, but the web/text medium, reducing bodily input to the mere tapping of a keyboard, allows little or none, especially given the poor grasp of prose style that most web warriors exhibit. So when you read yet another of those embarrassing blog conversations of the "All the people I hate are Nazis!" sophistication, ask what the discussion might have looked like if the conversationalists had been in the same room with their chosen targets. The more that human relationships play out in the disembodied world of the web, the more superficial and unnuanced they will be; and a generation will grow up that is cheated of the true joy of knowing the meaning of real friendships.

Second, bodies impose limits on us. Thus, in its virtual elimination of the body, the computer world offers users the potential (albeit illusory) of transcending their bodily limitations. On Facebook, I can be anybody I want to be: an eighteen-year-old Californian with six-pack abs, good teeth, a suntan, and a pilot's license; or even a 25-year-old blonde beauty queen from North Carolina with a degree in astrophysics. I can become the ultimate in self-created beings—a factor that, I am sure, also partly explains the massive, if little noted, popularity of role-playing video games in the modern world. In a virtual world, be it Facebook or the undersea city portrayed in Bioshock, I can be anyone I choose to be. I am the creator, or at least I have the potential to think I am.

How should the church respond? Well, the virtual world is new but it is here to stay; and it will no doubt continue to shape human behavior and self-understanding. We cannot ignore it but neither should we simply allow it to dictate to us who we are and how we think. Thus, we must teach people by precept and example that real life is lived primarily in real time in real places by real bodies. Pale and pimply bloggers who spend most of their spare time onanistically opining about themselves and their issues, and in befriending pals made up of pixels, are not living life to the full. Nor are those whose lives revolve around video games; rather, they are human amoebas, subsisting in a bizarre non-world that involves no risk to themselves, no giving of themselves to others, no true vulnerability, no commitment, no self-sacrifice, no real meaning or value. To borrow a phrase from Thoreau, the tragedy of such is that, when they come to die, they may well discover that they have never actually lived.

For myself, I rejoice that I grew up before the web and the video game supplanted the real world of real friendships, real discussions, real lives. I did not spend my youth growing obese and developing Vitamin D deficiency in front of an illuminated screen, living my life through the medium of pixels. However she does it, the church should show this generation of text and web addicts where real friendship and community lie, not with some bunch of self-created avatars on Facebook but with the person next to them in the pew on Sunday, with the person next-door, with the person they can see, hear, touch, and, of course, to whom they can talk, and who is created not in webworld but by the mighty Creator. And never, ever allow your church to go virtual so that people think that logging on to a service or downloading a sermon is really being part of the body of Christ. Of course, I write as a self-proclaimed miserable middle-aged git. My instinct, therefore, is that things like Facebook, along with low-rider jeans, dances that involve the "splits," and sentences such as "It was like you know like totally awesome and stuff," are probably best left to the under-25s. Use these web doohickeys if you must; just don't mistake them for real life, or the relationships that only exist there for real friendships. As for me, I'm simply going to continue sitting in that metaphorical dingy motel room, a cigarette hanging from the corner of my mouth, a glass of bourbon on the bedside table, bashing out copy on my typewriter.

Listening to Janis Joplin the other day, I was struck by two things. First, my eleven-year-old son (who had never, to my knowledge, heard Joplin) commented as he heard the first bars of "Me and Bobby McGee" that he didn't know I had a Joplin album. To recognize the voice like that at 11 must make him a blues-rock prodigy.

Second, I suddenly realized why I liked her (and, remember, she did win "The Ugliest Man of the Year" contest at her high school). It's the Lutheran lyrics of Bobby McGee: "Freedom's just another word for nothin' left to lose." Surely this captures the Lutheran notion of the freedom we have in Christ. OK, she may not have seen it (or Kristofferson who, I think, wrote the lyrics); but I'm sure Luther would have approved and downed a good German beer in her honor. Only when we realize we have nothing to lose because we are in Christ can we truly give ourselves in service to others. That's why Lutheran (and Protestant) ethics are really so demanding.

20

CELEBRATING THE DEATH OF MEANING

October 2009

IT HAS BEEN A GOOD couple of months for the celebrating of life at memorial services. First, there was the celebration of Michael Jackson's life, and then there was Ted Kennedy, enfant terrible turned elder statesman. Both men, in their different ways, were proof positive that, in modern America, you only need to love your own kids and then at some point die in order to atone for any sins you may have committed against other people's beloved sons and daughters. Yet even at these "celebrations" there are embarrassing moments when reality either breaks in or it takes a real act of will to ignore it. With regard to the Jacksonfest, as one media pundit put it: "You know you're in trouble when someone has to use the phrase 'Everyone is innocent until proven guilty' at your memorial service." And everybody knows what was the skeleton in the cupboard at the Kennedy memorial. As Elvis Costello once sang, "It's the words that we don't say that scare me so."

What I found most striking about the deaths of these two men was the language that was used by the media, language that raised a whole host of questions in my mind. In particular, both deaths were described as tragedies, a hackneyed term, I am sure, but still interesting in this context. After all, people die every day and no one describes their deaths as tragic. Does this mean that one has to be rich, famous, and talented/weird to die a tragic death? I confess that the whole idea is rather perplexing, reflecting the same hierarchy of life that laws about hate crimes embody. I have never understood why the teenager who kills someone because of the color of their skin or their sexuality should be treated any differently by the courts from the one who kicks to death the homeless man on the street. Does the lack of identity politics, a lobby group, and electoral significance render a street dweller's life of any less value? I have similar concerns regarding the practice of allowing victims' families to speak to the judge and jury in open court before sentencing: does the murder victim with no friends or relatives to speak for him thereby deserve less of a voice and less justice?

But there is more. The idea of death—any death—as a tragedy is surely, by terms of contemporary discourse, also something of an anachronism. While debates about the precise nature of tragedy and the tragic rage on in academic circles, it is generally agreed that for some event to be tragic, it must be set against an overall background of meaning. On these terms, the death of the modern also signals the death of tragedy, for the loss of meaning is surely one of the things that truly separates the modern from the postmodern. To read works by Joseph Conrad, Franz Kafka, Andre Gide, Albert Camus, and even

Samuel Beckett, is to read works that surely present a picture of life as confused, futile, absurd; but behind it all, there is a belief that somewhere there is a meaning to the grand scheme of things, even if that meaning is unknown and inaccessible to the protagonists. In *The Trial*, Joseph K may have no idea what crime he is being charged with or why; but the assumption throughout is that he is being so charged and that somebody, somewhere, knows the reason why. The same is true for the poetry of the later Yeats or of T. S. Eliot: to say that the center cannot hold means that there must be a center; and the hesitant, frustrated banality of Prufrock requires that there must be a greatness, a transcendence that he cannot seem to achieve.

> I have seen the moment of my greatness flicker
> And have seen the eternal Footman hold my coat and snicker,
> And in short, I was afraid.

When modernism despaired of finding that meaning, whether as a result of Auschwitz or postcolonialism or Derrida or Jerry Springer or simply skeptical boredom, it also just as surely dismantled the possibility of tragedy and evacuated the language of tragedy of any meaning.

This is where these ridiculous "celebrations of life" come into play. Now, I have in the past regarded such things as horribly sentimental, a classic American attempt to make everything have a happy ending. And, boy, Americans do like happy endings. I remember my jaw hitting the floor some years ago when I watched a Disney version of *Notre Dame de Paris* where the Hunchback does not die but lives happily ever after. I suppose I should have been grateful that the Americanization of the story was somewhat incomplete in that Quasimodo did not also have corrective surgery that turned him into a Brad Pitt lookalike—although there is still time for a sequel, I guess.

Even so, the point of the story of Quasimodo is that the guy with the hump dies at the end and it is all terribly sad. My wife is meant to cry, and I am meant to feel angry at the raw deal Quasimodo has been dealt in the poker game of life; to take that away is to change the storyline beyond recognition. I mean, imagine King Kong where the monkey sees the error of his ways, climbs down the Empire State Building, follows the Seven Spiritual Laws on How To Become a Better You by Not Kidnaping Blonde Actresses, and goes on to win *Dancing with the Stars*. A happy ending, and surely much to be desired from the monkey's perspective; indeed, a heartwarming story of triumph over adversity. But, let's face it, the story would lose a certain something.

Is "celebrating the life" of a dear, departed simply symptomatic of this sentimental vacuousness at the heart of our culture? Is it merely a postmodern reversal of Little Orphan Annie's song that finds a happy ending in the recollection of the sunrises of all our yesterdays rather than in the hope that the sun will come out tomorrow? I am sure that, to some extent, this is the case; further, in the case of celebrities, I am sure that making death into one last performance is also a factor, although that perhaps applies less to the celebration of life for the likes of most of us. As Evelyn Waugh commented in his novel *The Loved One* in the late 1940s, "Liturgy in Hollywood is the concern of the stage rather than of the clergy." Replace

"Hollywood" with "the modern Western world" and the statement is more true now than ever before.

But I also think there is more to it than this. It also represents an acknowledgment that meaning has died. In a world that denies there is any transcendent storyline to life, accessible or inaccessible, we are, as we are repeatedly told by the postmoderns, left to create our own meaning, our own stories, our own significance. Gone are the gloom and doom of Conrad, Eliot, Kafka, and Camus: gloom and doom depend on some meaning out there somewhere; after all, you have to have something about which to feel gloomy and doomy, don't you? This is where death is such a problem. Every fiber in our being tells us that, when a loved one dies, it is terrible, significant, devastating; yet how so, when there is nothing about a life that transcends the life? How does one go about creating a meaning for it? Not by looking to the future, as to resurrection, which is where the Christian would look. No. There is no resurrection nor even reincarnation. And as death itself is, in the memorable phrase of Wittgenstein, not an event in life, one cannot find its significance there. Thus, it is only by ignoring death and celebrating life that, paradoxically, we can give death meaning. I say "paradoxically" because in the very act of celebrating the life of the dead one, we acknowledge that we can find death's significance only in its insignificance. It signifies nothing. If life were really meaningful, the last thing we could ever do was celebrate it in the context of death. Death would then truly be a tragedy, and no celebration could even be attempted. Instead, of course, we focus on what remains—or rather, what does not remain. There is no response to a meaningless boundary other than an act of defiant nostalgia.

171

And in this death of meaning, even the nostalgia itself is a veritable fiction. The writer, Katherine Anne Porter, comments in her *Notebooks* that "[o]ne of the most disturbing habits of the human mind is its willful and destructive forgetting of whatever in its past does not flatter or confirm its present point of view." Go to the typical celebration of a life and you see this willful amnesia in spades. The Catholic Church, even with its new, consumer-driven fast track to sainthood, still takes a few years to confer the prize on the lucky three-times miracle worker. But the secular world goes for canonization as soon as the first speaker at the "celebration" picks up the mic.

Thus, a moderately talented dancer and OK singer who hadn't made an album that even his fans thought was up to much for the last twenty years, and was also clearly a very disturbed and tormented middle-aged weirdo, becomes a godlike talent of surpassing innocence; and an old man who, if he had been either you or me, would have done hard time behind bars and never been put in charge of a cleaning roster at the local Old Age Pensioner Tea Dance, let alone legislation in the most powerful country in the world, becomes an elder statesman. That he did good work as a legislator is arguable; that, if his name was Smith or Jones or Trueman he would never have been heard of, is incontestable.

To celebrate life at a funeral or memorial service is nonsense. It is an insult to the bereaved relatives who, at best, are surely only kidding themselves that the death is made somehow easier by the fact the life was worth living in the first place. Surely that makes the death even less of a context for celebration. It is also a ridiculous contradiction in terms:

if life has meaning, then death is an outrage; if death is not an outrage, then life has no meaning. In either case, what is there to celebrate? And those of us who believe that life has a meaning have even less cause to celebrate than those who are narrating themselves into their own storylines. Let's keep funerals for grieving and lamentation at the outrage that sin has perpetrated on the world. Keep the happy endings for Disney's sugar-coated castration of classic fiction.

21

MAKING EXHIBITIONS
OF OURSELVES

April 2009

I HAVE DRAWN ATTENTION to the phenomenon of Facebook—that (to me, anyway) weird Internet sensation where everybody and anybody can connect to (or, to use the jargon, "friend") anybody else in the world of virtual chatter; and I argued that, among other things, it witnessed to a world where privacy was no longer considered a virtue, and where everything had to be flaunted for all to see.

Well, I was shocked a couple of weeks ago to switch on my television set one Saturday morning and see the frightful Jade Goody staring at me from the box. For those who do not know, La Goody first came to fame a few years ago on the British voyeur series, *Big Brother*, where a group of self-absorbed misfits live in a house together, watched by continual video cameras streaming their antics to a television audience (or "peeping toms" as they used

175

to be known). La Goody was, I confess, quite a laugh, becoming famous for her stunning ignorance, such as speculating about the location of "East Angular." Some years later, she appeared on *Celebrity Big Brother*, a version of the same vacuous "social experiment" (or "freak show" as it used to be known), but this time with a group of misfits drawn from the pages of *Hello* magazine or the social pages of *The Sun*. This time, it was not so much her American-level knowledge of geography as her racist abuse of a fellow inmate that landed her in hot water. Finally, she appeared in the Indian version of *Big Brother* to prove she was no racist ("Some of my best friends are . . . ." Well, you get the picture). Here she received the news—on air as it happens—that she had terminal cancer.

Overnight, she enjoyed public redemption, and became a very public face for a very horrific disease. A life that had seemed to represent the worst vacuousness and stupidity of British society became significant in drawing attention to women's health issues, to cancer, and to the reality of the fact that young lives (I believe she was 27) can be cut tragically short for no apparent reason. Weeks before her death, she married her boyfriend; and she sold her story, etc., etc., this time not for personal gain, but simply to make sure that her two young sons would be financially secure after the death of their mother. In the public's eyes at least, a good death atoned for a previously pointless life.

Now, before I go further, let me make it plain that the death of a young mother is a tragedy. Children lose the person they love most; a partner is left alone; parents are bereaved of a beloved child. Jade Goody's death was no doubt deeply sad for those who knew her, and who loved her, and whom she loved in return. There is no question or doubt about that. What was bizarre, however, was the dramatic outpouring of public grief by people who did not know her at all, as witnessed by the scenes along the route of the funeral, the endless TV coverage of the event and its aftermath, and the newspaper and web treatment of the same. What is going on in Britain?

The parallels with the death of Diana, Princess of Wales, in 1997, were striking. There again a young mother died a pointless death, and children were orphaned. And, my oh my, wasn't there a spontaneous outpouring of public grief. Coming not so much from the stiff-upper-lip side of English culture as from the "everything I need to know about getting in touch with my feminine side I learned from watching D. I. Jack Regan in action in the seventies police series *The Sweeney*," the Diana-grief phenomenon was a mystery to me and left me cold. I wanted to mow the lawn during the funeral, but my wife banned me from so doing. What would the neighbors think? Yet the grief was all so over the top and cringeworthy—whether it was the mass weeping on the streets of London, the meaningless title "Queen of Hearts," the people who flew in from California "just to be part of it," Sir Elton John singing at the funeral, or (most incomprehensible of all) the comment by one Scotswoman on the BBC News that she was "going to find it very hard to go back and live in Arbroath after this" (hey, Arbroath may have its faults, but there are worse places...). The whole thing looked tacky, embarrassing, superficial, and contrived.

But what was truly fascinating was the false intimacy of the whole thing. Part of me watched the Diana grief fest and wanted to scream out, "Don't you people have any real problems to worry about? Have you never been really bereaved of a true loved one?"

Now, as I said above, the death of a young woman is a deeply sad event; but it impacts her children and her close loved ones in a way that it does not impact those who never really knew her. After all, what had most of those who grieved lost? Nothing. A collection of electronic pixels on the television screen. An image. A photo in a magazine. Somebody who was no more real to them in practical terms than James Bond or the Tooth Fairy. Yet the media had convinced people who had never met her that she was an important and intimate player in their lives.

The same applied to Jade Goody. History repeated itself: a likable but undeniably dim and virtually talentless woman and loving mother was struck down in her youth, leaving behind two orphaned boys. A very sad happening. But for whom? Is the sadness not trivialized by the way in which vast numbers of others with no real connection to the deceased muscled in on the family's grief, and used the idioms of mourning and bereavement?

Yet the false intimacy of the deaths of these women was no doubt a function of the way they had chosen to live. After all, they went out of their way to make exhibitions of their lives at every opportunity. No one could forget the secret visits that Diana made to the poor and the sick, where the cameras were (coincidentally) always there to capture the event for posterity and *Hello* magazine; and Goody took all this to the next level, being a contestant on multiple *Big Brother* shows and then having the rapid violence of her final illness catalogued in painful color for all to see. There were even rumors that she had arranged for her death to be filmed. These proved untrue, but that they seemed credible at the time is indicative of the culture she represented and to which we all now belong.

Much is written these days about the surveillance society, about the fear of having "them"—usually the government—watching our every move and thus restricting our freedom and invading our privacy. Ironically, with the rise of celebrity culture, the crass confessionals of the *Oprah* show and its amateur equivalents on Youtube, reality TV, blogs, Facebook, and now all the twitterati on Twitter, it is we who have destroyed privacy and have collapsed the difference between what is public and what is private and what is worthy of attention and what is mindbogglingly trivial. Apparently, we love it and cannot get enough of it, if the news headlines and websites and the direction of capital investment on television shows is any indicator. If you've got it, apparently, then you should flaunt it for as many people to see as possible.

The results of this kind of culture are clear and unpleasant. In our world of exhibitionists, a sense of entitlement rules the day. Everyone with a webcam or a modem has a right to be heard or seen saying or doing whatever they choose. Standards of basic decency disappear: the mainstreaming of pornography is only the most obvious example of the cultural erosion of the notions of what is and is not decent public behavior and the closely related concept of privacy. As both Diana and Jade indicate in their separate ways, style inevitably triumphs over substance, and the beautifully or shockingly mediocre beats hard work and talent every time.

But, perhaps worst, all sense of what is important goes out the window, especially in the realm of human relationships. The most extreme example of this is death itself. When thousands of people who never knew Diana or Jade, and were never even affected by them in any way other than a warm fuzzy feeling they would get when looking at their pictures on TV—when such people, I say, can break down and weep at their deaths and use language of personal bereavement to describe their feelings, then true mourning and grief and bereavement have been reduced, if not to nothing, then certainly to next to nothing. What is worse, because they did not know the bereaved, then whatever the rhetoric they use, the bottom line is that their mourning is all about them and not about the one who has died or about those who are truly bereaved and left distraught at the graveside.

If relationships with others are to be at all meaningful, then they need to embody levels of privacy, and concepts of decency and modesty. To be truly bereaved requires that one is first truly intimate or connected to the person. My relationship with my wife is unique; that we do not have sexual relations with others, or flaunt our own for others to see, is vital to the reality and importance and uniqueness of that relationship. The same goes in different ways with friendships and other human relationships. Privacy, decency, modesty are critical, and the levels of these in each relationship determine the nature and importance of that relationship. The whole culture of modern media, from television to Internet, is designed to put strain on, if not completely abolish, these basic concepts that are so important. Dare I suggest that one of the battles of the next decade for Christians is not so much how we can use the new media for spreading the gospel, but how we can stop the new media from destroying those things that seem so germane to the normal Christian life as the Bible envisages it, where people matter more than pixels and, no, not everybody has a right to know and see and do everything.

Last summer, I stood by my father's coffin. There were only eleven of us at the funeral: my mother, myself, my two sisters and their partners, my oldest niece, and Dad's two brothers and their wives. It was just as Dad had instructed: a private, modest, and decent affair with nobody present except those who really cared; no tears except those drawn from wells dug deep into the lives we had shared with him over many years; no stranger there to trivialize the moment by trying to steal a share in our grief. We grieved truly, and still do every day.

But where are the thousands who lined the route of Diana's funeral, or even those of Jade Goody? Already they have moved on to a new website or tabloid headline or reality TV show. For them, everything changed; and then, two days later, it was back to business as usual. In my mind, however, I remain standing by my father's coffin.

22

The True Repentance of an Inconvenient Jester

September 2010

SOME MONTHS AGO, a Presbyterian magazine criticized a response I had made to comments about me by a certain well-known writer in a popular Christian publication. My response, the writer declared in good, contemporary fashion, was unfortunate because it contained "jesting, which is inconvenient" and handled a "senior figure" somewhat roughly. The writer clearly thought prose that used the occasional bit of humor was far more reprehensible than the original accusation of slander by said "senior figure" to whom I was responding. That's "slander" as in "misrepresentation with malice aforethought of a person's actions with a view to damaging their public reputation"—apparently a fairly trivial accusation as far as my Presbyterian chastiser was concerned. After all, the accusation of slander was, if false, merely a breach of the Ninth Commandment and nothing like as serious as a bit of "inconvenient jesting"; and, if having any substance, not a charge one would want to bother making in the appropriate, procedural fashion, involving charges, specifications, a fair ecclesiastical trial with a chance for the defendant to clear his name and all that sort of bleeding-heart liberal malarkey. What a waste of time and effort that would be. As to the rough handling of this "senior figure," I guess I must apologize: all I can plead is that, at the time of writing, I was not aware that observing the Ninth Commandment or the decency and order of due process was unnecessary once one had a bus pass and a pension book.

Still, I was grateful to the writer for one thing: the timely reminder that serious sense-of-humor failures are, in Protestant circles, if not exactly compulsory, at least something highly to be desired, a good metric for judging sanctification. And that was sufficient to bring me to my moral senses. Thus, I am happy to report that this particular inconvenient jester is now, if not a thoroughly convenient killjoy, at least well on his way to becoming such a one.

I should have known, as a goodish Protestant, that all humor in theology serves a wicked purpose. After all, it is the papists who produce the funniest writers, from Newman to Chesterton to Waugh, with even Walker Percy having his moments. Need I say more? Can I rest my case at this point? To put it in logical form: Catholicism is bad; Catholicism has produced funny people; therefore, funny people are bad. Thus, given the religious provenance of its best exemplars, humor must therefore be intrinsically evil: if they make you laugh today, then, by good and necessary consequence, we know they'll be forcing you to kneel down and kiss the pope's ring tomorrow.

In comparison with Catholic wit, Protestantism has clearly been far more sanctified. While Spurgeon was definitely a master of the one-liner (hey—nobody's sinlessly perfect this side of glory), and Kierkegaard a master of irony (but no orthodox person reads him today, on the grounds that Francis Schaeffer told us he was a naughty boy), Protestantism has thankfully produced very few decent humorous prose stylists. In fact, just to be on the safe side, Protestantism has actually produced few decent prose stylists of any sort, for that matter. Indeed, I suspect one would have to go back to Jonathan Swift to find a broadly orthodox Protestant churchman who was able to write sustained, elegant prose that still proves capable of provoking laughter. And he wanted to eat Irish babies, didn't he? Now, I love Irish babies, but I could never eat a whole one. We can be grateful, therefore, that polished Protestant prose more or less died with the dean, and we are now free to enjoy the more godly, less ambiguous, and certainly less jesting prose of modern-day wielders of the Proddy pen, from Peretti to LaHaye. How convenient is that?

Of course, there were early attempts to destroy the essential godliness of Protestantism. Martin Luther was particularly reprehensible in this regard: making jokes about how much he drank, and about farting in the face of the Devil; mocking that poor, hardworking, sincere preacher who spoke at length on the virtues of marital sex at a service held in a home for elderly single ladies—pace Martin's condescending sneers, many of the old ladies found it "very deep," or so I am told; and as for telling his wife in love letters about how many bowel movements he was having in a morning while away from her, words fail me. But then, as a repentant inconvenient jester myself, such failure should, I suspect, be a source of some personal comfort and encouragement. Indeed, to extrapolate, it is surely a cause for rejoicing, as we look at the wider Christian world, that Luther seems to have ultimately made so little impact on contemporary Protestant church life.

Calvin was, thankfully, fairly humorless most of the time, although we should be cautious about ascribing this to pure godliness—no hagiography, please, we're Calvinists after all! In fact, I imagine that the great (the greatest?—in a non-hagiographic way, of course) saint's humorlessness was, in part, one of the few benefits of the severe bladder stone problems and other health issues from which he suffered throughout much of his adult life. Still, even he had his moments of sinful and disappointing weakness. The famous satirical inventory of relics is a case in point. If you read it after drinking a couple of glasses of red wine and filling in your tax return, it can indeed provoke laughter; but this is just sad testimony to the fact that even one of the great and the good like Calvin can on occasion exhibit unfortunate Romish tendencies.

As to John Owen, when it comes to satire the man was a virtual crypto-papist, making it incomprehensible that he still seems to enjoy such vogue among those otherwise concerned with jesting that is inconvenient. OK, his early attempts were generally over-the-top misfires, a bit like any American knockoff of a British comedy you care to mention, and thus safely devoid of anything approaching clever humor. Case in point: the description of free will as some pagan idol in *A Display of Arminianism*; but then he really hit his stride in the 1650s. Just read his Socinian Catechism—God having a body, sitting in heaven, wondering what might happen tomorrow? Didn't he realize these were serious issues with which he was dealing? And how hurtful and counterproductive this mickey-taking of admittedly absurd theology was to senior figures among the Socinian movement, senior figures who, one might add, would surely not have taken kindly to such rough handling by a pre-pubescent theologian in his late thirties? Was this satire likely to win such to Jesus? I don't think so, Johnny Boy. Straight to the detention room and write out "I must not have fun ridiculing silliness and its advocates" four hundred times, please!

This is one reason why it is so good to be alive today. The greatness of contemporary Protestant evangelical literature and church life surely lies in the fact that it is, by and large, so godly as to be utterly humorless and, on frequent occasion, beyond parody. Novels that talk of the end times, where every Arab and almost every European is wicked, and never use words of more than three syllables; blogs that witness the modern-day posturing of the Little-Endians and Big-Endians as they do battle over vitally important topics such as coffee machines and single malt Scotch—it's all very encouraging, really. As Wordsworth wrote of the French Revolution, so one might today respond to the literary culture of Protestantism that has placed itself bravely beyond the reach of satire: "Bliss was it in that dawn to be alive, But to be young was very heaven!"

Indeed, when you think of the dangers of humor, it is a very good job that the Protestant church today is not burdened with the likes of Luther, Owen, Swift, and even Spurgeon. Humor, after all, implies that the world in which sin and evil are rampant is somehow absurd and not the way it should be. Ridiculous. It also hinders us from understanding that our opponents really are dangerous and powerful in an ultimate sense and that our conflicts with them are of cosmic proportions. Nonsense. That's why fools like Luther used to laugh at their opponents, as if, in doing so, he might somehow convince himself not to fear those who destroy the body but rather him who has the power to cast body and soul into hell. So silly. Above all, it might prevent us from taking ourselves too seriously, and stop us from realizing that, yes, it really is all about us, and that we are indeed the meaning of the universe. That's why Luther rabbits on about his bowel movements: it is in part a constant reminder of his mortality and, frankly, the absurd, earthy, undignified, and ridiculous thing that humanity is in this world of countless towers of Babel, golden calves, and creatures strutting around with "Worship me! I'm the Creator!" tattooed on their chests.

So, when you sit down tonight and pick up your copy of *Really Serious Piety* by the Rev. Ichabod Horatio Morticius (Convenient Press, 2008), raise a glass to modern Protestantism, both orthodox and radical, to sense-of-humor failures everywhere, and to the idolatry of ourselves to which all this po-faced piety—traditional, Emergent, and all points in between—witnesses. The last thing the church needs is more jesting. That would be far, far too inconvenient.

This month's *Reformed Man Today* is well worth a purchase. As well as having a rather fetching picture of Mark Dever on the front looking a little like Tom Cruise in *Top Gun* (as they might have said in the sixties if they had had access to time travel, those reflecting glasses are so eighties, daddy-oh!), it also includes an interview with Derek Thomas, musing on his time as head roady for classic Wolverhampton rockers, Slade, in the seventies. In a more pensive moment, however, he does make the following philosophical observation about humor: "Things aren't funny in a world where there are no rules. Humor is about creating a tension that is resolved in an unexpected way etc. Does this mean that our humorless reformed brothers are closet postmoderns?" Interesting point. I had just thought they had no life, but if this is true, it could reshape the confessional landscape. I think we should be told. As Slade's own Noddy Holder might have said, "I just don't know why, anymore, anymore . . .."

I BLAME JEFFERSON: A DISSENTING VOICE ON LAUSANNE III

November 2010

THOMAS JEFFERSON was no orthodox Christian, but I have a deep suspicion that he should take significant responsibility for one of the greatest myths that currently dogs the church in the modern world. In drafting the Declaration of Independence in 1776, he helped to create the impression that declarations and petitions can actually achieve something. Certainly, he was proved right in the eighteenth century, but that was not because the declaration in itself was singularly potent; rather, it was part of a complex of factors that precipitated the American Revolution and thus saved the British from the tedium of baseball, American football (use of feet optional), and sausages that are apparently made out of the material used on the back of carpet tiles.

Seriously, the declaration is perhaps the greatest example of both the power of petitions and the pungency of political prose in the history of the world. The problem is that it has left a residual belief in the wider world that petitions can achieve something.

This belief seems to exert a peculiar hold over the minds of many Christians, despite, I should add, all of the evidence to the contrary. Indeed, the last few years have seen a number of petitions and declarations that have all, by and large, achieved nothing. One example was the online petition organized to oppose the transfer of an openly gay, ordained Church of Scotland minister from one presbytery to another. The petition garnered a large number of signatures but failed to stop, or even to delay, the move. The reason was obvious from the start: churches, particularly Presbyterian churches, operate according to strict rules of procedure; a petition has no procedural standing in the courts of the church; and therefore it is essentially irrelevant. Anyone who has any experience of church courts will know that procedure trumps mere conviction and sheer volume every time.

The Manhattan Declaration is another example. While the Church of Scotland petition was designed to achieve a certain specific immediate end, the purpose of the Manhattan Declaration was both broader in scope (as it addressed more wide-ranging cultural issues) and more nebulous in terms of its immediate ambition (as it was not aimed at a particular piece of legislative action). For all of the excitement surrounding its launching, however, and the high hopes that it would have some kind of significant impact, it seems to have achieved almost nothing in the time since it was published and, perhaps most ironically, served in certain evangelical quarters as a source only of discord. Evangelicals typically make the fatal mistake of assuming that the wider world cares about what they think. It does not: it increasingly regards us as fringe lunatics, rather as it did in the first century.

With this in mind, I look with some skepticism at the outcomes of the latest Lausanne gathering in Cape Town. Of course, in so doing, I am aware that I immediately open myself to accusations of being a killjoy, a naysayer, a Reformed Andrei Gromyko, the Soviet foreign minister who was known simply as "Mr. Nyet" at the United Nations. Given that this gathering has already produced the first part of a document that advocates things as unexceptional as loving God and neighbor, and wanting to see more evangelism, it is hard to criticize without appearing mean-spirited. So let me say at the outset, I am very much in favor of loving God, Father, Son, and Holy Spirit, and consider evangelism to be a very good idea. It is not these things that concern me.

What puzzles me is the idiom by which these things are expressed. Do we really need a "declaration" on these things, and what good is this actually going to do? First, I might remark that, frankly, such sentiments as "We love God" and "Jesus is unique" are in a similar league of obviousness to the phrases "We oppose wife beating," "We consider clean water to be a good thing," and even "Disco music was a very bad idea (not to mention the white suits and chest wigs)." To read some of the blogs and reports on the conference, you would think that something new and radical was being proposed. Nothing I have seen could not have been found better expressed elsewhere by somebody else at some point in the past.

The question then becomes: Did we need a gathering of thousands of church leaders (although no leader from my own church, local or otherwise, seems to have been present), at huge expense, to tell us these things? Do most of us not belong to churches where such things have been part of the very reason for our existence from the very start? The conference presumably cost hundreds of thousands of dollars to organize (if not more), before one even includes the hours spent by said church leaders away from the local postings to which they have been called. Is this a legitimate use of money at a point in time when many churches and Christian organizations are struggling to make their budgets? This is not to make a naive argument that the money should simply have been doled out across the world (we would all have gotten sixpence, I would guess), but it is to argue that, if the investment is so great, we should expect a decent return; yet statements of the obviousness of a typical pikestaff, albeit couched in dramatic prose, scarcely qualify.

Second, I wonder what ongoing status the new documents will have. To be brutal, a church document only has significance if there are penalties appended to it in the event of a breach. Thus, if I were to deny the virgin birth, I would be tried and prosecuted on the grounds that I was breaking my ordination vows, which bind me to maintaining the system of doctrine of the Bible as expressed in the Westminster Standards. Lausanne covenants have no such canons attached to them. So what does it mean for an individual believer or church to affirm such a covenant? It is surely at best the expression of aspirations, of gospel ambitions; beyond that it has no significance. Now, the expression of such aspirations is in no way a bad thing; but we do need to remember that the expression of a set of aspirations is very different from commitment to a church creed or confession that defines a congregation or a denomination because the latter has judicial standing, and thus has a much more fundamental significance.

Third, I wonder about the way in which the gathering was constructed. Clearly, the Lausanne movement is not a church but rather an eclectic collection of leaders from various churches. It transcends individual denominations, but does so in a way that is simply not very ecclesiastical. Now, I know that we want to find ways and means of expressing our unity in Christ; but to do this via a non-ecclesiastical root is not consonant with Scripture and leaves the gathering vulnerable to the accusation that it is self-appointed and unrepresentative. This latter criticism is particularly ironic, given the laudable desire of the organizers to be inclusive and, to quote the web page, to be "perhaps the widest and most diverse gathering of Christians ever held in the history of the Church." To play the postmodern card: one wonders who decided which people were "representative" and thus received an invitation, and which were not and were left by the wayside.

Maybe Lausanne III will be significant. I wish I could believe that. More likely, I suspect, it will go the way of Lausanne I and II: it will produce some inspiring documents and an interesting book or two, and perhaps give those fortunate enough to have been present a vision of the kingdom that may last for a few months or maybe a year. It certainly will not have any impact at the local level: it does not have the mechanisms attached to it to do so. Thus, for most of us, life will go on as normal, in all of its boring, mundane routine: we will ensure that the gospel is faithfully preached week by week from our pulpits, we will attempt to apply God's Word to the routine pastoral problems of our congregations, we will seek to reach out to the community where God has placed us, and we will, in these straitened times, strive to meet our modest budgets. In this context, a context very familiar to most Christians, some of us will wonder whether the money and time spent in Cape Town might not have given a better return if invested elsewhere.

With the great demographic shift to the Southern Hemisphere in terms of evangelical Christianity, the issue of listening to the voices of brothers and sisters from these newly significant areas is a pressing one. But I want to raise some concerns.

1. Culture and geography are only two ways of dividing up the world and the church—ways that we can argue are increasingly arbitrary—and their very trendiness makes them attractive at this point in history. Yet class would seem to be just as significant. Calls for us to listen to voices from other parts of the world should not be used to crowd out the voices of the poor and the working class in the West.

2. The demographic shift may be to the south, but the economic power of Christianity lies stubbornly in America. This is significant for several reasons:

* It means that theological education, for better or worse, is likely to remain controlled by America (institutions, books, journals, magazines all require money—and if you don't have the capital, sheer numbers of people are less relevant).

* It means there is a very great danger of the old imperialism and paternalism of previous generations simply co-opting the language of cultural sensitivity while continuing with business as usual. Cultural sensitivity, like all cultural phenomena, can easily be processed through the three c's of the modern West: commercialization, com-

modification, and consumerism. When it does this, it ceases to be a critical force and becomes simply one more product in the cultural marketplace, internalized and emasculated. Thus, putting "Worldwide" or "International" in the title of an organization that is funded by Americans and basically run by Westerners does not make the organization truly international or worldwide. There seems to be a problem when church leaders give lectures on listening to brothers and sisters from the Third World when said leaders have never taken the time or had the courtesy to learn the languages of those to whom they claim to be listening, and who assume that this "listening" should self-evidently go on in organizations founded by—you guessed it—Westerners, funded by Westerners, and run by Westerners. There is a real danger here of paternalism: yes, we want to listen to you, but you first have to learn to speak our language and come to our conferences.

The answer? Well, I'm a Reformation academic. I could not credibly be so without being able to operate in four or five modern European languages (not well, but well enough) and a few ancient ones. It would be absurd for me to lecture my students on listening to, say, German scholars, if I could not read some German. I also have to attend, on occasion, meetings where the medium language is not English, and that are run by, say, the Dutch, the French, or the Germans. Those church leaders who are rightly called to lead us in listening to our Third World brothers and sisters but who wish to avoid looking like old-style imperialists need to show their commitment and integrity by backing this up with a few linguistic skills in the appropriate areas, and perhaps by surrendering their organizations and their status to these brothers and sisters. Only when such leaders learn a few relevant languages and sit humbly and quietly at conferences organized by "the other" will their words begin to possess that most elusive quality: authenticity.

24

IS HURT MAIL THE
NEW HATE MAIL?

July 2009

Y E A R S   A G O ,   I   T R I E D (and by general consensus failed)
to develop as my party trick an impersonation of the Hollywood
actor, Christopher Walken. When I donned his identity, I just
said the one line: "I'm going to hurt you." To anyone familiar
with Walken's films, the line, if not exactly sidesplittingly hilari-
ous, was supposed to be at least vaguely amusing. Walken had,
after all, made his career on the back of playing psychopathic
megalomaniacs whose sole purpose in life seemed to be to inflict
unnecessary pain on various hapless victims. As I have never been
a good mimic, however, I usually had to explain who I was trying
to impersonate, at which point whatever little strength the joke
possessed vanished like the morning mist in summertime.

That line—"I'm going to hurt you"—has come back to my
mind more times than I care to remember over the last few years

as the language of pain and suffering has come to permeate main-stream modern discourse. Everywhere I look, I find people "pro-cessing their pain," "feeling the hurt," or reacting to comments from others that are variously described as "hurtful," "insensitive," or "cruel." It would seem that the world is being overrun by the evil spawn of Christopher Walken, to whom the "hurting" and the "pained" are now responding en masse. I might even propose a new law, to go alongside that of Godwin's. Let's call it "Trueman's Second Law" (Trueman's First Law is known only to a few close friends, but, trust me, it has never been broken). Trueman's Second Law would be formulated something like this: in any exchange of views, sooner or later one or more of the participants will describe themselves as hurt or in pain as a result of somebody else's com-ment; and at that point it is clear that they have lost the real debate.

I confess that I have a serious problem with all this alleged pain and suffering because these terms and associated words are, by and large, being used in vacuous and trivial ways. What, for example, should I do when I receive a note from someone who claims to be "hurt" by something I have written that she described as a "personal attack," despite the fact that I have never heard of her and was completely unaware of her existence until she chose to contact me? Now, I am no philosopher, but it would seem to be logically necessary for me to know of the actual existence of somebody before I can launch a personal attack on the person. Thus, to respond as this person did would seem to point to one of two possible explanations: she was a narcissist and thus incapable of understanding that articles written by another could possibly not be aimed at her; or (and frankly, more likely), she was clueless about controversial discourse and unable to separate critique of a particular viewpoint from a malicious attack on any person who might hold to said viewpoint. Whichever was the case, however, the use of the language of hurt and pain as primary involved both a trivialization of those concepts in themselves and a sidestepping of the real issue, i.e., was the argument I proposed right or wrong?

Of course, in the current climate, such sidestepping is not really considered sidestepping at all. My readers will know that I beat the "postmodernism is aesthetics" drum with some regularity. By using the categories of hurt and pain with reference to arguments, one plays the ace in the postmodern hole and effectively focuses attention not on the substance of a position but on the style; or, perhaps more accurately, one transubstantiates the style into the substance. There has always been something of this in the nature of argument, of course: many of us have attended debates where our brains tell us that the one protagonist has won, but, frankly, he behaved in such an arrogant way that, when the votes are cast, we side with the loser and give him the spoils. But the modern world seems to have taken this to the next level: everything with which I disagree is so hurtful, every time I suffer a trivial setback I have to process my pain, and ethics and argument are all about aesthetics, not truth or falsehood.

The impact of all this feeling of hurt and processing of pain is twofold. First, as noted above, it transforms arguments from debates about truth into debates about taste, and that is lethal for Christian orthodoxy. Now, Paul does talk about aesthetics at points in his writings, and presenting arguments persuasively surely requires attention not just to what is said but to how it is said. But he railed something rotten against those who denied certain truths and proposed certain myths. Clearly, therefore, the current situation has gone way beyond Paul in its discounting of the content of arguments and discourse in favor of the packaging. The mewling and puking among the more aesthetically inclined over my comments on *Reformation 21* about the film *Milk* are a case in point: apparently, Christians can learn from the commitment of a homosexual activist to his cause, but they cannot and, indeed, they should not, learn from someone whose commitment to his cause leads him to decry the film as sleazy Hollywood propaganda, unfit for Christian consumption. In today's public square, it is apparent that plain speaking is unacceptably tasteless in a way that sanctimonious Hollywood sermons about the political radicalization of gay sex are not.

The second area of impact is the way in which this "hurt" and "pain" cheapen the language and lead to trivialization of all things serious. Late last year, I was sent a column from some web page where an individual was lamenting that he had lost his job. Now, I spent eighteen months out of work myself at one point in my life; it was not pleasant and I have great personal sympathy with anyone caught in such a situation. It quickly strips one of self-respect and dignity; but, believe me, bad as it was, it was not analogous to twentieth-century genocides in Europe. Yet this was the analogy this person drew and through which he apparently found the strength to carry on. Unemployment is depressing, but it is usually a function of impersonal economic conditions or personal incompetence, neither of which is the result of intentional maliciousness on the part of others, and it certainly bears no resemblance to seeing your male relatives herded into a field in Bosnia and machine-gunned to death.

The reason for this trivialization, of course, is that the idiom of pain and suffering places the individual at the center of the universe and makes him or her the measure of all things. It panders to the idolatry of fallen human nature. Suddenly, it is my experience, my feelings, and my pain that are the most important things. Sure, I have never known what it is like to see my loved ones gassed and cremated at Auschwitz, but I can be a victim too: I have lost my job, or been sworn at while driving, or had my opinions belittled in a blog somewhere. I don't know the pain of those who have really suffered—but my own trivial discomforts are just as important because I am me, I am the center of the universe as I know it, and I deserve to feel good about myself. To deprive me of this is simply cruel.

How did we get here? How did we reach the point where professing Christians can seriously compare a temporary experience of unemployment to organized genocide? How did things come to such a sorry pass that even in the church there are those who discuss theology not so much in the categories of truth and error but of hurt and pain? Well, postmodern monkey see, postmodern monkey do. My guess is that the church has come to ape the world; and before we all start thanking the Lord that we traditional, Reformed evangelicals are not like other men, this is not just a monopoly of the church on the left of the evangelical spectrum. Some of the biggest whiners, mewlers, and pukers out there are among the professed advocates of the old school approach to things. Thin skins, absurd senses of entitlement, and a bizarre conviction that all criticism of ideas is really a personally intended affront to those who hold them are not the exclusive preserve of any one theological party.

In terms of intellectual/cultural history, I suspect the fusion of Marxism and Freudianism in the late fifties and sixties in the work of men such as Herbert Marcuse made oppression less a function of economics and more of being forced to be "inauthentic" by society. This, combined with Freud's view of the subconscious and Marxism's false consciousness, meant that all disagreements could come to be seen as oppressive, and that, however plausible my arguments against your position might seem, they are really masks hiding my attempts to oppress or control you. Mix in Nietzsche via Foucault, and you have a heady philosophical cocktail indeed.

Few if any will have read any of these thinkers, but make no mistake: we live in a world that is reflective of the values they embodied and articulated. The importance of therapy in modern America is one key sign that the rarified philosophy of these men has penetrated in practical ways to the commonplace level of everyday life and routine. The net effects are evident everywhere: nobody can dare to say that their position is superior to anybody else's because that denigrates, marginalizes, represses, and oppresses. That therapy, conversation, and a general prioritizing of aesthetic categories now grip the church and its own moral and theological discourse should be a cause for real concern. In a world devoid of truth content, claims to truth are oppressive and thus personal, hurtful, and distasteful; and the church seems, by and large, to be buying into just this kind of namby-pamby nonsense.

But I think there is more to this phenomenon of hurt and pain than a mere aping of the culture. It is more cunning and dishonest than that. Over the last couple of years, I have noticed that the hate mail in my inbox has been replaced by what I now call hurt mail.

Now, the agenda of your typical hate mailers is pretty straightforward: they are simply attempting to intimidate or humiliate the recipient into silence. What you see is what you get. Hurt mailers, by comparison, are rather more subtle and duplicitous: by claiming pain, they immediately do two things. First, they make themselves the poor victims; and second, they imply that the targets of this hurt mailing are intentionally malicious perpetrators. The game is precisely the same as with hate mail—to make someone whom they dislike or whose opinions they discount shut up—but the tactic is different: to win by seizing the moral high ground that belongs to the professional victim.

This new tactic also involves a fundamental change in the whole moral landscape. Let's face it: pain, as an abstract concept, is not in itself evil or a sin. I run marathons: the training is painful, not to mention the races; but the personal reward at the end is worth it and unattainable without the pain; my dentist regularly causes me a certain degree of pain in order to save me from worse to come; and anyone who has endured cancer treatment can testify to the salubrious effects of physical discomfort. Nor is such good pain just physical: I hated leaving the security of the parental home, but I had to do it if I was to grow up; I disliked having my essays torn apart by my college tutor but it was the only way to improve my intellectual and literary skills; and parenting teenagers can be heart wrenching, but it has to be done. Pain in itself is not bad; rather, it is the cause or the purpose of the pain that provides the good or the evil involved.

Thus, to complain that somebody has hurt you is, as noted above, to put an aesthetic category where a moral category should be. The question to ask is not "Do I feel pain?" but "What has this person done that has caused me pain?" If the person has maligned you, trashed your good name, accused you of being cruel to nice old ladies and puppies with injured paws, then you may have good grounds to feel hurt. But the problem then is not the symptomatic pain that you feel but your accuser's actual transgression of a moral precept, in this case the breach of the ninth commandment. Don't whine about the effect; complain rather about the cause. Paul doesn't criticize others primarily for hurting him; he criticizes them for breaking moral commandments, for sinning against God.

Expressions of hurt are too often really something else: cowardly attempts by representatives of a cosseted and self-obsessed culture to make themselves uniquely important or, worse still, to bully and cajole somebody they dislike to stop saying things they don't want to hear or that they find distasteful. My advice to such is akin to that of the counselor in the Bob Newhart sketch: Stop it! If somebody's writing or speaking hurts you, ask yourself "Why?" Don't whine about the discomfort. Get a grip, get yourself some trousers, stop feeling sorry for yourself, and please, please, please, don't hide behind the aesthetic pietisms of the tiresome and clichéd "feel my pain while I process my hurt" posse. Have the backbone, have the decency—nay, have the honesty—to take your licks and move on, either to addressing the substance of the argument or to some area of endeavor that is, well, perhaps less painful and hurtful for you.

25

AM I BOVVERED?

SOME YEARS AGO a friend who had read something I'd written in an editorial for *Themelios*, having expressed approval of the piece, said to me, "What is it with you, Carl? Do you just not care that people hate you?" Well, that's a tough question to answer. Of course, there is a sense in which, no, frankly, I do not care. When you criticize someone, particularly in the American Christian world, where all disagreement is apparently seen as motivated by personal animosity and base motives, it is likely that they will dislike you. But such a feminized aesthetic is hard for a European of my generation to grasp, and even harder to respect. Frankly, if you can't stand the heat, you need to get out of the kitchen.

Constant criticism eventually hardens the hide. Looking back at my ever-increasing file of notes and quotes of love from fellow Christians, I see myself described therein as "a right-wing fundamentalist," then, somewhat paradoxically, "that Communist from Great Britain," "a non-Christian," "a very dangerous young man" (I was quite pleased with the "young" bit in that one), "Machen's warrior child" (strange, isn't it, how this hackneyed cliché drips so easily and frequently from some of the nastiest and most sarcastic blogs and websites in today's evangelical world?), "a wolfman who devours little children" (!?), and, less melodramatically, "a danger to children" (well, at least to homeschooled children, apparently), and, most concise of all, "evil." I even had one lady form a prayer group to "pray that God's judgment will fall on the House of True-man." I know about that because she had the courtesy to fax the seminary to ask whether it could be advertised on the student notice board. When telling my wife and kids about this over dinner (in case you were wondering, the praying lady was not the present Mrs. T), my oldest son put his hand on mine and said, "Don't worry, Daddy. I don't think the Lord will believe what she tells him about you." I was touched, although a little concerned that this comment's slight ambiguity might indicate incipient open theist tendencies in my offspring.

So hatred can often be like water off a duck's back, particularly when it comes from the wacko fringes, left and right, of the Reformed world. Yet there is, of course, always a level at which hatred and bile hurt. The saying about sticks and stones hurting bones but words never doing so is nonsense. You don't have to engage in the lunatic excess of some strands of postmodernism, where all reality is turned into a linguistic construct, to be nonetheless convinced that there is a sense in which words are a constituent, creative part of our world. When some stranger takes exception to something I've written and e-mails me to tell me I am an idiot or a child abuser, it hurts. When my kids tell me I'm not a good father, it hurts. When my wife tells me I've let her down at times, it hurts. The claims may be referentially true or false but that is scarcely relevant. Whatever the case, they construct a certain reality, and make a certain state of affairs come into being, whether I like it or not. As one of Catherine Tate's characters would say, "Am I bovvered?" Well, if I'm honest, yes, at some level I am, even by the most absurd and obviously untrue accusations. After all, somebody out there believes that some silly accusation is the case for them, it is a reality; and knowing this, I find that their reality impinges on mine. To call me an idiot may be idiotic, but it can still make me feel like one.

This is yet again where I find that giant of Protestant theology, Martin Luther, to be a singularly useful source of personal help and pastoral insight. Much ink has been spilt over Luther's theology, and I am guessing that most articulate evangelical people probably know that he argued for justification by grace through faith. They probably also know that he placed the preaching and hearing of the Word of God at the center of Christian piety. And, they probably understand that these two things are connected: the word of promise is believed by the individual who is then justified by grace through faith.

What has all this to do with the problems caused by words that create hurt or are spiteful, words that reshape our realities in ways that do us harm on numerous levels? Much in every way.

Central to Luther's Reformation theology was his understanding of how words constitute reality. He was helped in this both by his theology and by the immediate intellectual background from which he emerged—a background that I believe enhanced and facilitated his understanding of Scripture. To put it simply, Luther emerged from a medieval philosophical tradition that accented the reality and the power of words and that had come to drive something of a wedge between things and words, stressing the latter as constructive of what was known. He also worked against the background of a theological tradition that, through its emphasis on the all-powerful will of God, shattered the connection between the way the world appears to be to human beings and the way God necessarily and actually is. Just because certain rules seemed to apply in the created world (e.g., to be called righteous, one first had to possess the intrinsic quality of righteousness), did not mean that God was bound by such. In other words, reality—real reality—was exactly what God declared it to be.

Two particular instances of this are constructive. Creation is the obvious example. There was nothing; God spoke; now there was something. God's act of speaking was supremely powerful and creative. It generated created reality. In commenting on Genesis 1:15, he says the following:

> Here attention must also be called to this, that the words "Let there be light" are the words of God, not of Moses; this means that they are realities. For God calls into existence the things which do not exist (Rom. 4:17). He does not speak grammatical words; He speaks true and existent realities. Accordingly, that which among us has the sound of a word is a reality with God. Thus sun, moon, heaven, earth, Peter, Paul, I, you, etc.—we are all words of God, in fact only one single syllable or letter by comparison with the entire creation. We, too, speak, but only according to the rules of language; that is, we assign names to objects which have already been created. But the divine rule of language is different, namely: when He says: "Sun, shine," the sun is there at once and shines. Thus the words of God are realities, not bare words.[1]

1. Martin Luther, *Luther's Works*, vol. 1, *Lectures on Genesis: Chapters 1–5* (Saint Louis: Concordia Publishing House, 1999), 21–22.

He speaks and it is so! God's word is creative power of an unimaginable kind, utterly definitive and determinative of reality.

The other instance is the cross. The death of Jesus on the cross looks just like the hopeless death of a despised failure, and probably a criminal to boot. To one who does not listen first to God's words, it can only be evil. Yet God says it is not so: the cross is the power of God to salvation. The cross's reality is not constituted by what it appears to be, by what human categories and human words would say that it is to be; rather it is exactly what God says it is, nothing less than the glorious triumph of a gracious and holy God over all the powers of evil on behalf of fallen humanity; and human speech about the cross, if it is to be true speech, must correspond to the prior action of God. Luther makes this point most famously in the Heidelberg Disputation of April, 1518. Thesis 21 and Luther's explanation of it read as follows:

A theologian of glory calls evil good and good evil. A theologian of the cross calls the thing what it actually is.

This is clear: He who does not know Christ does not know God hidden in suffering. Therefore he prefers works to suffering, glow to the cross, strength to weakness, wisdom to folly, and, in general, good to evil. These are the people whom the apostle calls "enemies of the cross of Christ" [Phil. 3:18], for they hate the cross and suffering and love works and the glory of works. Thus they call the good of the cross evil and the evil of a deed good. God can be found only in suffering and the cross, as has already been said. Therefore the friends of the cross say that the cross is good and works are evil, for through the cross works are destroyed and the old Adam, who is especially edified by works, is crucified. It is impossible for a person not to be puffed up by

211

his good works unless he has first been deflated and destroyed by suffering and evil until he knows that he is worthless and that his works are not his but God's.[2]

Finally, this power of divine speaking culminates in justification. Luther understands that God does not find men and women righteous and then declare them to be so as some act of description of, or response to, an established state of affairs. Luther knows that God declares that which is drenched in sin, foul, obnoxious, and deserving of nothing but divine wrath—Luther, I say, knows that God declares this person to be righteous; and by the sheer power of the divine word, they then are righteous. This is no cosmic gas or mere legal fiction, as some have claimed; rather the divine word makes it so. It is the word that establishes the death of the old, the birth of the new, the reality of the status of the child of God as blessed and beloved of the Father. Human beings are passively righteous; but what active, practical passivity is this. To quote contemporary Lutheran theologians Robert Kolb and Charles Arand:

> The passive righteousness of faith . . . frees me from what others say about me, for what they say is not the final judgment, but is always provisional. For faith believes God's gracious judgment despite all empirical evidence to the contrary. In other words, we cling to the promise regardless of how many times instant replays of our weaknesses and failures pass before our eyes.[3]

2. Martin Luther, *Luther's Works*, vol. 31, *Career of the Reformer I* (Philadelphia: Fortress Press, 1999), 53.

3. Robert Kolb and Charles P. Arand, *The Genius of Luther's Theology* (Grand Rapids: Baker, 2008), 50–51.

Others might tell me I am a failure, an idiot, a clown, evil, incompetent, vicious, dangerous, pathetic, etc., and these words are not just descriptive: they have a certain power to make me these things, in the eyes of others and even in my own eyes, as self-doubt creeps in and the Devil whispers in my ear. But the greatness of Luther's Protestantism lies in this: God speaks louder, and his Word is more powerful. You may call me a liar, and you speak truth, for I have lied; but if God declares me righteous, then my lies and your insult are not the final word, nor the most powerful word. I have peace in my soul because God's Word is real reality. That's why I need to read the Bible each day, to hear the Word preached each week, to come to God in prayer, and to hear words of grace from other brothers and sisters as I seek to speak the same to them. Only as God speaks his Word to me, and as I hear that Word in faith, is my reality transformed and do the insults of others, of my own sinful nature, and of the evil one himself, cease to constitute my reality. The words of my enemies, external and internal, might be powerful for a moment, like a firework exploding against the night sky; but the Word of the Lord is stronger, brighter, and lasts forever.

Gentlemen,

On behalf of the Campaign for Real Thoughtfulness (CRT), I write to request the return of Carl Trueman to your blog. On behalf of the vast, silent majority of humorless Reformed types in this world, and as a representative of two significant Reformed organizations (World Alliance of Christian Know-all Obnoxiousness

Societies [WACKOs] and the Campaign for a Humourless and Uninteresting Christian Universe of Publications [CHUCUP]), I am writing to beg you to reinstate Carl Trueman on the blog. Frankly, I miss his uninformative, unfunny, unhelpful, childish contributions (which, incidentally, are of a standard that would have been barely acceptable at high school). Please, please, please, make him return—only when you publish such drivel do we give our young people an excuse to be so ill-equipped for later life, and am I able to become truly outraged, and then write in to Ref21, feel important, and parade my own humorlessness as some kind of divinely ordained virtue. So please, bring Trueman back; we need plonkers like him to give really important people like me something to complain about. If you don't, then there will be no place for WACKOS or CHUCUP on your web page.

26

IS THE THICKNESS OF TWO SHORT PLANKS A FORGOTTEN DIVINE ATTRIBUTE?

May 2010

NONE OF THE systematic theologies I own include "being as thick as two short planks" in their treatments of the divine attributes, but it appears that there is a trend today to rectify this neglected aspect of God's being. Bear with me while I explain.

I remember while at Cambridge in the mid-1980s, a cartoon appeared in the university student newspaper depicting weirdy-beardy students from the Sidgwick Site (the home of the Arts faculties), with the caption "The world is text; we move from sign to sign." The point was twofold: first, to poke fun at the pretentious jargon of those for whom every other word was "semiotic" or one of its cognates. Such were apparently spending their time at college in an effort to learn how to state the obvious using language that completely obscured pretty simple ideas, and to do so in tones such that even the most banal statement might sound like a profound and groundbreaking insight. Most have, presumably, gone on either to teach in university Arts faculties, where their inability to communicate would be considered a strength and not a weakness; or to write those easy-to-follow manuals for IKEA flatpack furniture and Eastern European digital cameras.

The second point of the cartoon was to ridicule the notion that life could be reduced to language, a very trendy position at the time and one that is taking a terribly long time to die. Without going into the ins and outs of the theory, I have often wondered, for example, exactly how helpful it is to think of the Holocaust as "text" or a "linguistic construct." It may be that we need words to talk and write about such a thing, but instinct seems to indicate that there has to be more to it than that.

Words are interesting and powerful, no one denies that. And one of the ways this is made clear is that there are so many struggles about words and how they are used. Indeed, "political correctness" is, if nothing else, a movement about language: the disabled become "differently abled"; various racial epithets are outlawed, if not by the state then at least by the bounds of acceptable taste and convention; and, indeed, in striking a blow for that despised group, the middle-aged male bald guy, I might suggest we replace "baldy," "chrome dome," "Mekon" (hey, that last one will test your knowledge of postwar British pop culture), and "helmet head" with "follicly challenged," "alternatively thatched," and the increasingly popular self-designation "Mature, intelligent male with youthful outlook and GSOH seeks lady (20–25) for friendship and perhaps more."

There is, however, another aspect to the changing of language that is driven not so much by a desire to avoid hurting others but rather by the attempt to hide the full horror of certain situations. We are all aware of how this can be done. Sometimes it is done with reference to things that are not necessarily evil but that are not exactly good news: to close a loss-making factory might be "to rationalize resources"; to put a sick dog out of its misery might be "to put it to sleep." Other times it can be clearly utilized to blunt or even invert the moral dimensions of an action: to argue for abortion is to be "pro-choice"; to kill off the elderly and the infirm is "euthanasia" or "mercy killing" or "death with dignity" (however one dies, I suspect the departure of life from a body can never be dignified, just more or less awful).

Well, so much for the way in which language has been used in general public discourse; what is really worrying is that some of this spin is now firmly established within the church. Two recent examples come to mind. First, there is the notorious case of Ergun Caner, of Liberty Theological Seminary. Caner allegedly invented whole swathes of his past in order to enhance his public profile and career. Most normal people would regard a cock-and-bull story concocted about growing up in Turkey and having a background in jihadi culture, if not actually true, then as being a pack of lies put forward for personal gain by playing on American evangelical fears about Islam. Not so, according to Elmer Towns, dean of Liberty's School of Religion, in a statement to *Christianity Today*: if Caner's story is not true, then it is just a case of the kind of "theological leverage" in which the school typically allows its faculty to engage.[1]

So telling lies has now become theological leverage, and is acceptable once one has reached a certain rank in the Christian

1. *Christianity Today* (May 2010), accessed August 22, 2011 at http://www .christianitytoday.com/ct/2010/mayweb-only/28-11.0.html.

firmament? "What?" you say. "Next thing you know, they'll be inventing new and trendy terms for adultery that blunt the moral force of that sin too, presumably not an ethical matter either, providing one is high enough up the evangelical hierarchy to be accountable to no one." Well, funny you should mention that . . . recently, I happened to come across someone talking about a new sin with which I was not familiar, the sin of relational mobility. Hmmm, I thought, sounds interesting. I wonder whether that's what it's called when I roll over at night and accidentally whack my wife on the head with a flailing arm as I fight off some imagined sea serpent that has invaded my dreams? Or perhaps it's a cute way of referring to the typical husband's capacity for vanishing off the face of the earth when his wife wants to go the shops to choose some new wallpaper?

Wrong on both counts. As I investigated the conversation, the crime in question seemed to be nothing less than divorce based on adultery: to be blunt, the shattering of a marriage by illicit and explicit genital intercourse between two people outside the bonds of the marriage vows that had been taken. That's what the sin of "relational mobility" apparently is. Nice way of putting it, n'est-ce pas?

There are a number of things to notice about these two incidents. First, they typify the trendy obfuscation that has increasingly dogged our societies for twenty years or more. It reminds me of another Cambridge cartoon, depicting a scientist telling a friend that his dog had just died, or, to quote his words exactly, "entered a permanent mode of negative functionality." Thus it is with pompous flannel: to call the telling of lies "theological leverage" or to describe the straightforward destruction of a marriage by the sexual betrayal of a spouse as "relational mobility" is a good, if obviously gutless and sleazy, way of hiding exactly what it is that has been done.

Second, as regards "relational mobility," it is interesting that the language itself was spouting from the lips of someone who seemed to need to cast everything from God to garbage disposal systems in "relational categories." Yet, while the language used the word "relational," it actually served to depersonalize, derelationalize the whole thing. Tell me you've committed adultery, and I know you have had sex with someone you shouldn't, and thereby permanently damaged your relationship with your spouse, the one you promised to love, come hell or high water, because, like some sexually incontinent rabbit, you couldn't keep it in your trousers. Tell me you've committed the sin of relational mobility, and as far as I am concerned, you might simply have hit the neighbor's fence post while parallel parking. Adultery carries long-established weight that highlights exactly the sexually explicit nature of the betrayal of a loved one; "relational mobility" is vacuous, self-serving, sleazy flannel.

Third, and not to put too fine a point on it, it's so utterly dishonest and completely bonkers, worthy of inclusion in the Encyclopedia Dissemblica under the entry for "Pretentious Jargon Used by the Sleazy to Avoid the Consequences of Their Actions." I cannot wait to see the new, evangelical translation of Matthew 5:27 for the emerging market: "I say to you that everyone who looks at a woman with mobile intent has already committed relational mobility in his heart." That certainly packs a punch over against older translations. And we'll need to add a clause to the ninth commandment to the effect that it only applies to those who don't

FOOLS RUSH IN WHERE MONKEYS FEAR TO TREAD

hold positions of responsibility in the church or won't profit by their perjury—sorry, their "theological leverage."

What is so jaw dropping in all this is the clear belief of the people who use this language that the rest of us are complete idiots. If I built my career on telling people that I had grown up in the jungles of Borneo as the devoted worshiper of the Snake God and, after years of eating missionaries, had finally been converted through the ministry of one, I would be guilty of lying, not theological leverage, and everyone would know that was the case. And if I have had sex with a woman who is not the lady listed on my marriage certificate, I have committed adultery. My next-door neighbors know what adultery means; the mailman knows what adultery means; and quite possibly the man who stands at the local bus stop and talks to the fire hydrant, convinced it is his long-lost brother, might still have enough about him to know what adultery means. They can tell the difference between self-serving, dishonest flannel, and the truth. Am I alone in finding it offensive that these people who lay claim to being leaders in the church think that the rest of us are so stupid that we cannot see this for the patronizing dishonesty that it is?

Worse still, of course, are the theological implications: to think that I am an idiot is one thing. Many have done that; it's not unusual and, sadly, I am sure there is plenty of evidence to suggest that I am not the sharpest knife in the drawer. But these people seem to think they can fool God with their slick talk and sound bites. Yes, believe it or not, they apparently regard themselves as cleverer than their maker. Like Adam and Eve sewing fig leaves together in the Garden, they believe that, if they use the right words, he just won't notice the reality that lies behind their thin veil of semantic scamology. In fact, they have squeezed God into a box that is so small he barely has the divine equivalent of two brain cells to rub together. Their a priori theological system has led them to assume God is as thick as two short planks, and that a bit of obfuscatory language and the odd specious euphemism will prevent him from holding them accountable for their lies and the filth of their personal lives.

To consider other human beings to be so stupid as not to see through flannel about "theological leverage" and "sins of relational mobility" is patronizing and offensive; but to assume God is a moron, as thick as a brick, is, frankly, dangerous. Make no mistake: unlike the evangelical and Emergent dupes out there, God is not mocked.

Glossary

Banger. An old, beat-up car.

bovvered. Phonetic spelling of the way Londoners and slovenly teenagers pronounce the word "bothered."

Brummy. Somebody from Birmingham. That's Birmingham in the U.K., not Alabama, although the latter is the only place in the U.S.A. as attractive as the English original.

bum. A person's seat, rear, or backside.

cheese rolling. An ancient Gloucestershire sport that involves a crowd of people racing down a very steep incline (Cooper's Hill), chasing after a round cheese. This is a highly dangerous sport, so there are usually teams of medical staff at the foot of said hill to deal with the inevitable injuries. The winner is the one who captures the cheese. The prize? The cheese, of course. Footage of the event can be found at http://www.cheese -rolling.co.uk/2011_yoho_media_cheese_rolling_video.htm.

dodgy. Sketchy (clothing); not quite kosher (general); heterodox (theology); containing salmonella (kebabs, curries).

dosh. Money, moolah. Example: "He was trousering lots of dosh" means "He was making lots of money."

fob off. To give a substandard answer simply because one can do so. Examples: any sentence uttered by a politician in response to an interviewer.

git. Irritable person, usually of British derivation. Typically used of one of the four ethnic groups against one of the others.

Glaswegian navvy. A man or very tough woman from Glasgow who digs canals or works on other heavy excavation projects for a living.

Mekon. The leader of the Treens, creatures from the northern hemisphere of Venus who were the implacable enemies of British astronaut hero Dan Dare in the 1950s weekly comic, *Eagle*. The Mekon was easily recognizable for his complexion (bright green) and his head (massive and completely out of proportion with his body). His aim was to subjugate the solar system to his will. If he were ever to be portrayed in a Hollywood movie, he would thus have an English accent.

mewling. Crying. A term used by Shakespeare's Jacques in *As You Like It* to describe infancy, the first age of man. It still describes the first age of man, although this now extends to age 32 in most young people as opposed to Shakespeare's time, when it was strictly limited to preschool development.

mickey-taking. Poking fun at; laughing at. Verbal forms include "to take the mickey," "to take the mick," and, for the truly sophisticated, "to extract the Michael."

m'lud. Term of address used by English barristers when addressing a judge. Example: "The church's collection money was simply resting in my client's private savings account before it was to be put to work, m'lud."

Noddy Holder. Curly haired frontman of British 1970s glam-rock band, *Slade*. Hits include "C'mon feel the noise!" and "Goodbye to Jane." Platform shoes, flared trousers, top hats, long hair (after an ill-advised "skinhead" moment), limited musical talent, but loud and oh-so-cool. You get the picture.

numpties. Scottish word for plonkers.

pikestaff. A tall weapon that is immediately obvious when brandished. Only the dead and the stupid could miss it, with the latter soon joining the former as a direct result of their lack of observation skills.

plonkers. English word for numpties.

po-faced piety. That form of godliness that roots sanctification in the steady mortification of one's sense of humor and zest for life. Often manifested by a failure to see the lighter side of oneself, or of anything else for that matter.

Proddy. Colloquial word for Protestants, an extinct religious group that once considered the Reformation to have something useful to say.

pulling in the punters. Attracting customers in order to boost revenues; attracting congregants to boost the rev. . . . Errm, I mean "to extend the kingdom." Ahem.

[to] rabbit on. To talk incessantly. Popularized by pub rock duo Chas 'n' Dave in their classic contribution to Western musical culture, "Rabbit, rabbit, rabbit," notable for its fascinating syncopation.

shouting the odds. Expressing one's opinion in a way that does not show due deference to anyone else. A tell-tale sign that someone is about to start "shouting the odds" is that he invites you to "join the conversation" and then begins sentences with phrases like "With all due respect . . . ," "I hear what you are saying but . . . ," and "I am actually quite hurt by . . . ."

tighty whities. White Y-front underwear. Very uncool and unattractive, although still popular in many parts of Wales and Liverpool, I believe.

tosh. Rubbish. Examples: all of postmodern theology; books with the word "revisioning" or "reimagining" in the title; any sentence that contains references to "feeling pain" where no physical discomfort is involved, or to a "journey" where the speaker is not alluding to an intentional physical movement between two geographical locations.

DISCUSSION QUESTIONS

Chapter 1: Fools Rush In Where Monkeys Fear to Tread

1. What irony is described at the beginning of this chapter (1–2)?

2. What does true humility look like? What example does the author give (5)?

3. What is "greatness by proxy" (5), and how is the mention of "my mate, Kev" (5), an example of it?

4. T. E. Lawrence struggled with his attitude regarding public acclaim (6). How are many people like Lawrence in this way? What makes most people ultimately different?

5. What does the author believe Christians should avoid doing online (7)? How can they promote the good and true without promoting themselves?

6. The Internet facilitates the "phenomenon of the self-blurber" (5). How might this phenomenon manifest itself in other areas of life? What is the fundamental problem?

Chapter 2: The Crowd Is Untruth

1. What were the author's reasons for reading Søren Kierkegaard (10)? What is the danger of letting others do your thinking for you?

2. Is it necessary to "come to the point of despair" (14) to have true faith? Why or why not?

3. What is the tension between the individual and the larger body of the church (12–13)? What is meant by "One must first believe as an individual before one can belong to the community" (14)? What would this look like on a practical level?

4. "American individualism feeds directly into this negation of the individual" (14). What does this mean? How does this happen?

5. The author maintains that "the church in America seems to have the worst of both worlds" (15). What are these worlds? What is the solution?

Chapter 3: Messiahs Pointed to the Door

1. What is the function of celebrities in American culture? How does this express itself in sports (18)? In politics (19–20)? How is the British approach different from the American approach?

2. In what ways is American politics Pelagian (21)? In what ways is it Manichean (21)? Why are these views simplistic (21–22)?

3. What forces are more powerful than the individual politician (21)? Why do Americans put too much hope in their politicians (20–22)?

4. How does the "cult of the individual celebrity" (18) translate into the American church (23)? What examples of this have you seen?

Chapter 4: The Nameless One

1. What specific "shortcomings and potential pitfalls" (26) of the Young, Restless, and Reformed (YRR) movement are mentioned in this chapter?

2. "History is littered with the serious human wreckage caused when good Christian people start worshiping the messenger rather than the One to whom the message refers" (27). Can you think of examples?

3. How does the author define pragmatism (29–30)? Is pragmatism always wrong? Why or why not?

4. The author writes, "The routine of the ordinary, the boring, the plodding, is actually the norm for church life" (30–31). Is this true? What characterizes your church's life? What are signs of a healthy church?

5. What will prove that the YRR movement is timeless (31)?

6. What is the difference between wanting to teach and wanting to be a teacher (32–33)? How can orthodoxy be heresy (33)?

Chapter 5: Pro-Choice Not Pro-Options

1. What is the "cult of options" (36)? What are some examples from today's culture?

2. If "to lead is to choose" (35), how might the cult of options undercut modern leadership? What is problematic about the "language of conversation" (37)?

3. "Sometimes, it is better to make a decision that proves to be wrong than to make no decision at all" (39). Do you agree? Under what circumstances might this be true?

4. What is meant by the phrase "Statesmen are made, not born" (40)? What is the downfall of "those who simply arrive on the scene" (40)?

5. How can people learn how to make decisions? What are some signs of a true leader (40)?

Chapter 6: The Freudom of the Christian

1. What is "Christian Freudom" (43)? How have the "trivial taboos of fundamentalism . . . become the trivial necessities of modern evangelicalism" (46)?

2. "Evangelicalism just isn't cool or hip or *avant-garde*, and attempts to make it appear so, whether theologically or culturally, always end up as self-defeating" (45). What attempts does the author mention throughout the chapter? Can you add others to his list? What makes these attempts so pitiful?

3. How was Christ's death "profoundly un-Freudian" (48)? What bearing does that have on the way Christians should live their lives?

Chapter 7: Look, It's Rubbish

1. What were some of the problems with the service that the author attended at the beginning of the chapter? Would you take a non-Christian to this service? Why or why not?

2. Why are orthodox academics concerned about their reputations in secular universities (54–55)? According to the author, how do liberals perceive "duplicitous conservative[s]" (55)?

3. How can conservative worship services be similar to the worship service described in this chapter (56–57)?

4. "The typical non-Christian . . . assumes a certain correlation between the seriousness of content and the seriousness of form" (54). How might Christians be tempted to compromise content? Why is this so reprehensible (57–58)?

Chapter 8: On Meeting Joe Frazier: The Missing Element of Modern Theology

1. Who will never worry about assurance of faith (63)?
2. "I am increasingly convinced that this loss of a burning sense of God's holiness is the problem of modern theology, modern biblical scholarship, and modern church life" (63). Do you agree? If so, what evidence have you seen for this loss?
3. How can Christians come to a better understanding of "God's terrifying holiness" (65)? What are some signs that they have overlooked it (65–66)?
4. According to Gregory Nazianzus, who should listen to discussions of theology (66–67)? Why?

Chapter 9: The Freedom of the Christian Market

1. What makes the free market fallible (72–73)? What assumptions about the market are "woefully naive and unmitigatedly Pelagian" (73)?
2. What drives the forces of history (71)? Who is to blame for the banking crisis (74)? Why?
3. Why should Christians be embarrassed to speak of "the morality of the markets" (75)? What is the danger of viewing the markets as moral (75–76)?
4. "We are all guilty" (76). Do you agree?

Chapter 10: From the Versace Vacuum to the Brand of Brothers

1. Why might someone use a pseudonym (81)? How is this different from using a ghostwriter (82)? How is using a ghostwriter different from turning the apparent author's name into a brand (82–83)?

2. How are today's ghostwriters "utterly separable from the author" (83)? Is this the same issue as the "death of the author" (83)? Why or why not?

3. What leads you to purchase a book? How does the author's name influence you?

4. What is the sign that we are "moving away from the acceptable canons of literary practice and intellectual ownership" (84)? Why does the author believe that this is so wrong (85)?

5. How can evangelicals fall prey to using "cultural idioms that are as worldly as anything out there" (85)?

Chapter 11: Welcome to Wherever You Are

1. What did the minister point out to the author (89)? Why was his observation so important?

2. Where are you called to serve first and foremost (91)? Does this seem limiting to you?

3. Why might the church be "best served by those with . . . limited ambitions and myopia" (91)? How can the Internet distract Christians from their true calling (92–93)?

Chapter 12: Why Are There Never Enough Parking Spaces at the Prostate Clinic?

1. Should Christians watch any movie they wish to watch (97–99)? Why or why not? What are your own criteria for watching movies?

2. According to the author, the need to hyperspiritualize everything broadens pietism instead of abolishing it (99). Why do Christians want to Christianize the things they do? Why might this be problematic?

3. "Talk about culture is talk about accidents" (100). What does the author mean by this? How can talk about culture be ultimately limiting for Christians (100)?

4. What happens when the church becomes "little more than a cacophony of competing voices" (102)?

5. "No one ever loses in today's evangelical market by backing the peripheral rather than the central" (102). What are some examples of this (102–3)? How can Christians reorient themselves in a trivia-prone society?

Chapter 13: Trapped in Neverland

1. "The world of my grandfather was evil because it made him grow up too fast; the world of today is evil because it prevents many from ever growing up at all" (109). What factors does the author blame for this (107–8)? Can you think of others?

2. Have you encountered people who view Christianity as a "refuge for the emotionally retarded" (111)? How would you answer someone who believed this?

3. According to the author, Blaise Pascal put his finger on the problem of human life when he saw how "entertainment had come to occupy a place, not as the necessary and momentary relief from a life of work, but as an end in itself" (111). Do you agree? Why might the author call this shift a "problem of human life" (111)?

4. Can you give examples of the emphasis that today's culture places on entertainment? What could be a sign that entertainment has become an end in someone's life?

5. What dangers come from having "wealth in abundance" (112)? Conversely, how did poverty shape the life of the

author's grandfather? Why do you think the author respects him so much?

6. "You are, of course, what you worship" (112). What does today's society worship? How can parents show love to their children without idolizing them or enabling their immaturity?

Chapter 14: An Unmessianic Sense of Nondestiny

1. The liberation of middle age comes from "match[ing] diminishing abilities and opportunities with diminishing ambition" (115). How is this view helpful? How might it be unhelpful?

2. The author claims that "most of us are mediocre" (116) and that "even our loved ones will somehow find a way to carry on without us" (118). Do you agree? How should this impact the way in which you view yourself and others?

3. "Far too many Christians have senses of destiny that verge on the messianic" (116). Have you met such Christians? Do you believe that this sense of personal destiny is problematic? Why or why not?

4. What is the author's view of church membership (118)? What does the role of an individual have to do with the role of the church?

5. How might a "certain unmessianic sense of non-destiny . . . make us better citizens of the kingdom" (119)?

Chapter 15: Old Opium Meets the New

1. "Culture is never value-neutral but is always part of a wider agenda" (122–23). What agenda do you see in today's culture? How might Christians buy in to this agenda?

2. "There are numerous other 'opiums' that distract people from the reality of their condition, material and spiritual" (123). Which three opiums are discussed (123–25)? What would you add to the list?

3. How does television "dull the senses of its willing victims" (125)? What makes it both dangerous and bland? What is its appeal?

4. "In our drive to be successful, there is still a constant temptation to judge our success by the criteria of the wider culture, to adopt the methods of the wider culture, and to co-opt the movers and shakers of the wider culture" (126). Can you give examples of how Christians succumb to these three temptations? How can these temptations be avoided or overcome?

5. How does the modern media "consume and subvert all that touches it" (127)?

Chapter 16: Reflections on Rome Part 1: Connecting the Mind and the Tongue

1. According to the author, Roman Catholicism has "everything American evangelicalism lacks—history, beauty, self-conscious identity, and, quite frankly, class" (130). Do you agree? What could remedy this problem for evangelicalism?

2. Which would the author rather spend an evening reading: "the typical evangelical offerings of [his] own tradition or some work by Aquinas or Newman or Kung or Ratzinger" (132)? Why? What Christian literature do you read, and why?

3. The author sees a disconnect between "the mind" and "the tongue" in Roman Catholicism (132). What does he mean by this? What incident drew this to his attention (132–33)?

4. "There is a fine line between credulity and skepticism" (135). Do Protestants ever cross this line? In the same way, how might Protestants be as pragmatic as Hans Kung?

Chapter 17: Reflections on Rome Part 2: The Need for History 101

1. How might a lack of knowledge of medieval architecture lead a Protestant to "metaphysical conclusions" (140) in Trento? What point is being made here?
2. What Catholic misconceptions did the author attempt to clarify throughout this chapter? What did he learn about priests of the Maronite Order (142)?
3. "We cannot even agree to differ with any integrity if we have not taken the time to learn each other's history" (143). Why does integrity matter in debate? Why is history so important to both Catholics and Protestants?

Chapter 18: Beyond the Limitations of Chick Lit

1. The author warns against relying on "Chick lit" to learn about Roman Catholicism (146). How do Protestants frequently characterize and mischaracterize Catholics? Where do Protestants get their information about Catholics?
2. What are the five areas in which the author believes Protestants can learn from Catholics (146–50)? Would you add anything to this list?
3. What are T1 and T2, and what is the difference between them (152–53)? Do you believe that the Scriptures are ultimately "complicated and obscure" or "clear and accessible"

(153)? How does your answer affect your understanding of authority (153–54)?

4. What central emphasis in confessional Protestantism prevents Protestants from having a "concessive attitude toward other religions" (154)?

5. How does a different understanding of justification result in different approaches to the sacraments (155–57)? Why does the author believe it is crucial that Protestants understand this difference (157–58)?

Chapter 19: No Text, Please; I'm British!

1. In what ways might the social-networking use of the word *friend* devalue the concept (161–63)? If you use social-networking media, what criteria do you have for choosing your "friends"? Are these the same criteria you use offline? Should they be?

2. The author writes, "Might it be that chat-show confessionals, navel-gazing personal blogs, and virtual social networks possibly stand in continuity with pornography . . . ?" (162). Why does he suggest this? What are the similarities?

3. How has the Internet redefined the concept of privacy and intimacy in today's society (162)? Are there any advantages to this? What are the disadvantages?

4. The author calls childishness "something of a textually transmitted disease" (163). How does Internet social networking reduce friendship to its more childish forms (163)?

5. The author identifies the "lack of the body in the means of communication and relationship" (163) as a key problem with Internet friendships. What arguments does he make to

support this (163–64)? How are bodily limits an advantage in a relationship (163–65)?

6. "We must teach people by precept and example that real life is lived primarily in real time in real places by real bodies" (165). How can we do this? How are real life, real time, real places, and real bodies important to Christianity?

Chapter 20: Celebrating the Death of Meaning

1. What, in your opinion, makes a death tragic? What makes a death tragic in the view of our culture (168)? What are some examples in this chapter of tragic deaths?

2. "The idea of death . . . as a tragedy is . . . something of an anachronism" (168). Why is this?

3. How does our craving for happy endings express itself at funerals (169–70)? What is the postmodern reasoning behind "celebrations of life" (171)?

4. This chapter concludes, "Let's keep funerals for grieving and lamentation at the outrage that sin has perpetrated on the world" (173). Should grief, lamentation, and outrage be the purpose of a funeral? In what way is that a Christian purpose?

5. Do you want your funeral to be a celebration of your life? Why or why not?

Chapter 21: Making Exhibitions of Ourselves

1. How was the public grief for Jade Goody and Princess Diana a demonstration of "false intimacy" (177)? Was it rational? How did publicity throughout their lives promote this response (178)?

2. When people grieve public figures they never personally knew, "their mourning is all about them and not about the one who has died" (180). What is real grief? What is its focus?

3. "The whole culture of modern media, from television to internet, is designed to put strain on, if not completely abolish," privacy, decency, and modesty (180). How does modern media affect relationships? How does it change our perception of bereavement?

4. Describing his father's funeral, the author writes that there was "no stranger there to trivialize the moment by trying to steal a share in our grief" (181). Can grief be stolen? What gives someone the right to mourn the death of someone else?

Chapter 22: The True Repentance of an Inconvenient Jester

1. "Serious sense-of-humor failures are, in Protestant circles, if not exactly compulsory, at least something highly to be desired, a good metric for judging sanctification" (184). What evidence do you see of this?

2. "Humor ... implies that the world in which sin and evil are rampant is somehow absurd and not the way it should be" (187). How does humor imply absurdities? How can it best be used?

3. What are the dangers of taking yourself too seriously (188)? According to the author, how and why did early Protestants avoid this (187–88)?

Chapter 23: I Blame Jefferson: A Dissenting Voice on Lausanne III

1. "The last few years have seen a number of petitions and declarations that have all, by and large, achieved nothing" (192).

Do you agree? Does lack of achievement render petitions pointless?

2. "If the investment is so great," the author writes, "we should expect a decent return" (194). What returns is he hoping for?

3. Is there a time and place for petitions and declarations? How might they accomplish something useful?

Chapter 24: Is Hurt Mail the New Hate Mail?

1. How is the transformation of "debates about truth into debates about taste...lethal for Christian orthodoxy" (201)? How does the apostle Paul prioritize style and substance (201)? How can Christians be alert to the difference between the two?

2. How do "'hurt' and 'pain'...lead to trivialization of all things serious" (202)? What example of this is given (202)? What examples have you encountered in your own life?

3. The "idiom of pain and suffering...panders to the idolatry of fallen human nature" (203). How? How do professing Christians come to this point (203)?

4. What are the differences between hurt mail and hate mail (205)? What are the similarities? How does hurt mail reflect a "fundamental change in the whole moral landscape" (205)?

5. When someone hurts you, what should you ask yourself, according to the author (205)? How might this help you to address your hurt in a Christian way (206)?

Chapter 25: Am I Bovvered?

1. This chapter states that the claims of others, whether true or false, "construct a certain reality, and make a certain state of affairs come into being" (208–9). How is this possible?

2. Martin Luther understood that "words constitute reality" (209). What two biblical instances of this does this chapter describe (210–11)?

3. How did Luther's view of the power of God's words affect his understanding of justification (212)? How does the author apply this concept to his own circumstances (213)?

Chapter 26: Is the Thickness of Two Short Planks a Forgotten Divine Attribute?

1. Words can be exchanged for others in an attempt "to hide the full horror of certain situations" (217). What examples are given (217)? Can you think of others?

2. What is "theological leverage" (217)? What is the "sin of relational mobility" (218)? Why might someone use these phrases (218–20)?

3. What does the use of such phrases say about the speaker's view of others (220)? Of God (220–21)?

ISBN: 978-1-59638-183-4

*P*olitics has become a joke. Sound bites and knee-jerk reactions have replaced reasoned debate. Isn't it time to think more deeply? Carl Trueman leads a readable, provocative, and lively romp through Christianity and politics.

"This historian-turned-pundit, with all the force of a prizefighter's left jab and right hook, leaves the left, right, and center (or centre) reeling on the ropes.... I heartily recommend that you read this book. But you do so at your own peril."
—**Peter A. Lillback,** bestselling author of *George Washington's Sacred Fire*

"Writing in a predictably provocative and forthright manner, Trueman pulls few, if any, punches. *Republocrat* is a timely and robust assessment of a vitally important issue and a *cri de coeur* for a reappraisal of the conservative church's current political alliance."
—**Derek W. H. Thomas,** Distinguished Visiting Professor of Systematic and Historical Theology, RTS; Editorial Director, reformation21.org